Inconsolable

HOW I THREW MY MENTAL HEALTH OUT
WITH THE DIAPERS

MARRIT INGMAN

Inconsolable:
How I Threw My Mental Health Out with the Diapers

"We're in This Together" originally appeared in *Crock: A Journal of Domestic Bliss* No. 1.

"Kid Rock" originally appeared in *Brain, Child: The Magazine for Thinking Mothers.*

"Playgroup Drinking Game" originally appeared as "The Lit Candle" on AustinMama.com.

"Me Against the Music" originally appeared as "Dear Trent Reznor" in *Mamalicious*, Volume 1.

"The Toddler Travels" originally appeared in *Clamor*, No. 27. July/August 2004.

Published by
Seal Press
An Imprint of Avalon Publishing Group, Incorporated
1400 65th Street, Suite 250
Emeryville, CA 94608

ISBN-10: 1-58005-140-5
ISBN-13: 978-1-58005-140-8

9 8 7 6 5 4 3 2 1

Library of Congress Cataloging-in-Publication Data
 Ingman, Marrit.
 Inconsolable : how I threw my mental health out with the diapers / by Marrit Ingman.
 p. cm.
Includes bibliographical references.
ISBN 1-58005-140-5
1. Ingman, Marrit--Health. 2. Postpartum depression--Patients--United States--Biography.
I. Title.
RG852.I54 2005
362.198'76'0092--dc22
2005011764

Cover design by Rowan Moore-Seifred, doublemranch.com
Interior design by Stewart A. Williams
Printed in the United States of America by Berryville
Distributed by Publishers Group West

TO SHEILA

CONTENTS

WHY I WROTE THIS BOOK

IN ONE OF ITS EARLY INCARNATIONS, the book you are holding elicited the following comment from an acquisitions editor: "As the mother of a daughter with reflux and motor delays, I can identify, but it's almost as unpleasant to read as it is to experience it."

Bingo, I thought. *I nailed it.*

She passed on the book, of course.

Writing this book kept me alive—creatively, spiritually, and literally—during the most difficult episode of my life so far. As you might expect from such a dire statement, this book is not uplifting, not redemptive, and not prescriptive, though these are the things we tend to expect from nonfiction about motherhood. We expect bromides and meditations, quips and moments of grace. We expect this even though there is technically no shortage of intimate personal accounts of early parenting: Anne Lamott's *Operating Instructions*, Jane Lazarre's *The Mother Knot*, Andrea Buchanan's *Mother Shock*, Ariel Gore's *The Mother Trip*, Rachel Cusk's *A Life's Work*, Susan Kushner Resnick's *Sleepless Days*. These books are "brutally honest" and "ring true" about "the dark side of motherhood." Yet the parenting section of your local bookstore will likely have one copy of one title. The rest of the shelf is choked with "expert" titles about how to soothe your fussy kid, how to get your figure "back," how to make your kid smarter with finger puppets and Mozart and fish oil. There are calendars and jocular self-help books and consumer guides. There is a plenitude of books for new fathers, usually with some bug-eyed cartoon dude freaking out on the cover, or else a celebrity dad smiling beatifically. *What a great guy.*

I pored through the mainstream, popular books when I was struggling with postpartum depression. *Where's the one for the crazy bitches?* I'd wonder. Sometimes I'd hit on a book that resonated through the haze of exhaustion and madness—Buchanan at one point realizes that if she were to jerk the steering wheel and crash the family car, her postpartum ordeal would be over—but mainly I'd leave empty handed. I'd have to go find a book that dealt specifically with mental illness, and few of these writers were mothers. They were post-grunge club kids or esteemed novelists or bipolar celebrities. Their depressions were glamorous and existential. They were not like me. I was too crazy to be a mother but too much of a mother to be crazy.

The other problem was that I didn't fit the model of the depressive mother advanced by the popular press. I wasn't dying quietly on the inside or crying behind my smile. I was screaming at my kid, who wouldn't stop crying, and beating up my walls. The expert books about "fussy" infants offered no answers—as did various doctors—but suggested an attitude adjustment for me. Why, I'd been given a precious gift! Why couldn't I be thankful and compassionate? I didn't need anyone to tell me I'd be great if I just carried the baby in a sling (which I did) or took my vitamins (which I did). I didn't want them to tell me the baby wouldn't cry if we slept with him (which we did) or nursed him on demand (which I did).

My husband, Jim, and I did everything we could think of, and we were still miserable until the baby started walking at fifteen months. And that, my friends, is the real reason I wrote this book: because there were no answers besides keeping my shit together any way I possibly could. And I knew there had to be other parents out there feeling the same way. Parents who weren't helped by expert books, well-meaning advice, or the family physician. Parents who wanted to yank the wheel every day. I wanted to talk to these people. I wanted to tell them they're not alone. I wanted to tell them they have a right to be proud of themselves. I wanted to tell them that when you're ready to stop being a tourist in your own life and really kick some ass on behalf of a small, screaming person, you're ready to be a parent. You are a good parent even if you feel angry sometimes, even if you feel angry often. You are a good parent even if you can't always stop your child's crying. You are a good parent even if you sometimes think you've made the biggest mistake of your life. You can be a good parent and still fight like cats and dogs with your partner, if you have one. You can be a good parent and still wear your pajamas all day. The only thing you have to do is fight as hard as you can. Some days it's good enough if everyone is alive at the end of them.

This book is for those parents. It is not for the sensitive and pastel among us. I do not recommend it for pregnant first-time moms with no depression or mental-illness history. (I frightened a pregnant receptionist once just by saying the words "postpartum depression" over the phone.) I do not recommend it if you're going to be bothered by the word "fuck" or by suicidal fantasies, or if you are feeling tender today and can't deal with someone else's rage. And I do not recommend it if, like that acquisitions editor, you expect reading about motherhood to be a consistently pleasurable experience. Why should it be? Motherhood is not consistently pleasurable, and mental illness is agony. We recognize that life's most intense and transformative moments can also be excruciating; yet despite the efforts of so many mother-writers, speaking about "the dark side of motherhood," whatever that means, is still taboo. I know for a fact that Andrea Buchanan gets loads of hate mail.

I wanted to deal with the "dark side" head on. My son will be growing up in a world full of negative shit. He'll probably beg me for a pair of sneakers sewn by nine-year-olds in Pakistan. What am I going to teach him by pretending that ugliness doesn't exist? He needs to know what it means to be angry, to feel destructive, to be frustrated, to feel self-hatred. Someday he may be the father of a child who cries all night. He may be the friend or partner or doctor of a depressed person. He needs to understand that his parents fought very hard for him, that we had to make ourselves love him and even each other, that we were sometimes tempted to leave him in a tree for bonobos to raise. I'm not afraid to tell him that I used to cut myself because I wanted to feel a kind of pain that I could understand and control. I'm not afraid to tell him that I wanted to drive our Volvo 850 wagon off the Highway 183 flyover. I'm not afraid to tell him that I used to put him down and close the door and scream and pound the wall until my hands were bruised. He doesn't understand yet, but he will someday. My greatest hope is that when he faces these feelings in his own life, he won't be afraid of them.

He'll know how to be strong and fight them. So, yeah, fuck that chicken soup shit.

A further note on the text: Throughout I will refer to my child by his *in utero* nickname—"Baldo." I named him after a baby raised by my characters in the virtual game *The Sims*. They were a cute lesbian couple who got a phone call from an adoption agency because they were making out all the time. While their "Baldo" screamed and squalled, they fell asleep on their feet and urinated where they stood. *That's funny*, I thought at the time. *Why don't they get any happiness points for tending to a baby?* (I was pregnant and not yet acquainted with the realities of infant care.) Then one day their "Baldo" suddenly metamorphosed into a brown-haired little boy in a soccer jersey, and he gave the Marrit Sim a hug. He began talking to her. Her happiness meter went off the charts. And so my fetus became "Baldo" as well. After the birth I learned that Saint Baldus is the patron saint of colic, so the name stuck.

I've chosen to use the name here because the baby in this book isn't necessarily the person my son really is. The baby is the person my son appeared to me to be when I was deranged and exhausted. I will assure you that he has since metamorphosed (though not as dramatically) into a bright, articulate person who no longer vomits on me seven times a day. He talks to me. He hugs me. We dance together to Soundgarden. And sometimes my happiness meter really does go off the charts. Sometimes I still fall asleep on my feet.

You take the bad with the good, I guess. This book is written from that standpoint. If you happen to be a depressed parent, parts of this book will likely be painful—perhaps "as unpleasant to read as it is to experience it." If that is true, my hope is that you will at least feel less alone. I can reassure you, however, that this book is ultimately about survival. I lost the person that I was, but I remade myself and lived. To look at me now, you'd probably never know I was mentally ill. I am a completely average and unremarkable neighborhood mom. My son is, in most ways, an average toddler. We are, in most ways, happy people, in part because we got to learn what unhappiness is. I believe this is possible for everyone; it's what parenting is.

WHAT DEPRESSION IS AND WHAT DEPRESSION ISN'T

WHEN MY SON WAS TWO YEARS OLD, his father and I each bought a ticket to one day of the Austin City Limits Music Festival, a weekend spree of live music and sweaty fraternity men held in a large municipal park. Jim wanted to see Cake and Elvis Costello on Sunday; I wanted to see Old 97's and The Pixies on Saturday. We would take turns attending the concerts and minding our toddler. Since mine was the Saturday ticket, it fell to me to chaperone one of his eighth-grade students, who was reporting on the event for the school paper. I was delighted to squire her around, give her journalism advice, and demur on her behalf whenever a joint passed our way in the crowd. Her mother provided our transportation to the event, where parking was limited. En route, I had the following exchange with a friend of their family, a man without children who was seated on the passenger side of their minivan:

Family Friend: A writer, huh? So what do you write about?

Me: Well, my current project is a memoir of postpartum depression.

Family Friend: Huh. That's hormonal, right?

Me: Perhaps partially. No one is sure. I'm interested in its sociocultural origins—the isolation of new motherhood, the feeling of having to live up to an impossible ideal.

Family Friend: I see. And that's a real thing? I mean, it's in the *DSM?*

Indeed, the *The Diagnostic and Statistical Manual of Mental Disorders*, a categorizing system advanced by the American Psychiatric Association, places postpartum depression in its Mood Disorders category, describing it as a major depressive episode with an onset within twenty-eight days of delivery. Most experts agree that this definition is too narrow, but it does *exist*, and thus postpartum depression is "real." As if millions of parents—mothers and fathers, biological and adoptive alike—couldn't tell you that.

So before I can tell you my story of motherhood and madness—before I can tell you about the sleepless nights and dreams of suicide and the wounds I caused myself—I must address the layers of myth and mystique surrounding "postpartum depression" as we understand and experience it. That way, you'll know it's all real.

The myth of postpartum depression (or PPD) is that your life is peachy and your baby is wonderful, but somehow you can't stop crying because your hormones went wonky after you gave birth. Levels of progesterone and estrogen drop after delivery, so maybe it's like that for some people, but it wasn't for me.

I suspect that when we talk about PPD, we're actually describing a variety of conditions, one of which may actually be the condition of motherhood itself. Some maternal depressions are situational in origin—from exhaustion, from emotional depletion, from being alone with a baby, from being supported inadequately. It's no secret that preexisting psychological disorders play a role, as do delivery and health complications, as does a lack of spousal or partner support.[1] In fact, you don't even have to give birth to get PPD. According to childbirth educator (and adoptive mother) Carol A. Hallenbeck, a depressive syndrome can be observed in adoptive parents.[2] Fathers can and do experience depression during the first year of a child's life. If the mother is depressed, the incidence of paternal depression can be as high as 50 percent.[3]

So maybe PPD isn't a malfunction of those mercurial female humors. Maybe it's more like a shitstorm parents endure because we are tired, frightened, isolated, confused, apparently powerless. Especially if we live in some stupid suburban family domicile without a strong community around us; especially if we have learned the lie that a parent looks into a baby's eyes and somehow knows exactly what to do.

"When you look into your baby's eyes for the first time, it will be the happiest day of your life," a relative told me when I was pregnant.

"You'll look into your baby's eyes and grow your 'mama spine,'" someone else said when I was confused about everything that confuses a new mother: circumcision, vaccinations, early-education curricula, whether to use cloth or disposable diapers, whether to tell my doctor to fuck off.

Maybe it's because I didn't get to look into my baby's eyes for a couple of hours after my caesarean. Then again, when I did I saw two narrow slits in an angry, red, screaming face. I did, of course, grow a "mama spine"—and I do believe that such a thing exists for everyone—but it was a long and difficult process, not instant and instinctive. It was many months spent pacing and soothing with qualified success, many long days spent crying in a chair.

Sometime in all this mayhem, I happened to see an episode of *The Ricki Lake Show*—yes, really—about PPD. The guests were different kinds of women: young and urban, thirtysomething and suburban. All of them believed they were failures at mothering.

"I just know she hates me," a Chicana mother with a fifteen-month-old insisted. "I only want to have a good relationship with her." She started crying uncontrollably, literally—the kind of sobbing where you get the hiccups if you try to talk.

I stopped joggling our son around the living room. Yes. Yes. That was it exactly. I could look at another person and think logically about her situation: *Of course she doesn't hate you. How could a fifteen-month-old hate anyone? You care for her. Of course you'll have a good relationship.* But when I turned back to my own child, I too felt like an abject failure.

"Failure" isn't the right word. Everybody feels like a failure sometimes, like an impostor in our lives and work. As if a perspicacious person could look right through the shell of who you are and see that you really know nothing about veterinary medicine or accounts receivable or double-crust pies or whatever it is you pretend to know something about in your life.

With PPD, you might feel as if you caused a person to exist and every moment of his or her life is misery. You have made life's biggest and most irrevocable mistake. You need to get the fuck out of here, and you'll do whatever you can—you'll put a gun in your mouth, you'll cut yourself—to stop the racing thoughts in your head, the ones telling you to put the baby down someplace safe and go gas yourself in the car, to get on the highway and go to another town so you can work some dumb-shit job and send money home to a kid who is better off without you in her life. You will fuck your child up if you stay. A stranger off the street could raise her better than you can, because you are sick—damaged, a liar, and a pretender. You are a piece of shit. Killing yourself would be a blessing to your child.

If you are fortunate, you will not become psychotic; you will not literally begin to believe that your child is in danger from something supernaturally evil and you need to smother her or drown her to keep her safe. But you know it's a possibility; you could slip into madness five minutes from now. Five minutes from now you may start hearing voices that aren't really there. How will you know the difference?

All new parents are sleep deprived. But even when your baby is napping, you lie there staring at the ceiling. Even in repose, your heart is racing, and it feels like someone is standing on your stomach. Sometimes you are bored. Sometimes you are anxious. You know you should rest but you can't.

Postpartum depression isn't the same as the "baby blues," when your hormones crash after delivery and you sweat like a pig, cry constantly, and collapse into a puddle. This is common and physiologically explicable. Postpartum depression is what happens next.

Postpartum depression is what happens when your brain becomes stuck in a state of misery. Whatever triggered it—isolation, stressful life events outside of mothering, diminished levels of progesterone and estrogen, thyroid malfunction—the feeling is the same. Like a virus or inflammation within the body, postpartum depression is an *observable disorder,* not a weakness in character or a flaw in logic. One cannot reason oneself out of it, just as one cannot reason oneself out of diabetes or hepatitis A.

According to the National Mental Health Association, the symptoms of postpartum depression are:

- increased crying and irritability
- hopelessness and sadness
- uncontrollable mood swings
- feeling overwhelmed or unable to cope
- fear of harming the baby, self, or others
- fear of being alone
- lack of interest or excessive concern for the baby
- poor self-care
- loss of interest or pleasure in activities (anhedonia)
- decreased energy or motivation
- withdrawal or isolation from others
- inability to think clearly or make decisions
- fatigue
- sleep disturbances unrelated to the baby's sleep patterns
- headaches, hyperventilation, heart palpitations[4]

Some researchers estimate the incidence of postpartum depression at about 10 percent—a figure that refers only to *biological moth-*

ers, not fathers or adoptive parents. Other studies suggest that PPD is more common, affecting up to 28 percent of biological mothers.[5]

Then there is postpartum stress disorder, which postpartum mental health expert Karen Kleiman describes as "an acute state of being overwhelmed and overloaded" (in other words, "early motherhood"). Talk therapy is indicated for postpartum stress, and behavioral changes are therapeutic: adjusting your expectations, setting priorities, receiving help with caring for your family.[6]

There is also postpartum anxiety, a term that describes the onset of obsessive-compulsive disorder, panic disorder, or generalized anxiety disorder after delivery.[7] Another anxiety disorder, post-traumatic stress disorder, is also observable in the postpartum period; for example, a woman's labor and delivery may trigger a response to a traumatic event in her past, such as sexual abuse.

Then there's postpartum psychosis: severe agitation, hallucinations, and delusions. This is the jackpot of postpartum mood disorders, affecting only one in one thousand women. Postpartum psychosis is a medical *emergency,* like cardiac arrest. It requires immediate medical attention.

Yet too many people simply don't believe in PPD, like the husband of a woman I met at a talk I was giving. "He says I have to make up for the past two years," she explained, as if she'd been delinquent instead of mentally ill. Other women in the room suggested that by that logic, he should "make up" for his body's various maladies over the years—including any instances of erectile dysfunction.

PPD is not a phantom ailment limited to married, middle-class women with "high expectations" of motherhood. Young mothers and single mothers are at statistically greater risk for PPD, as are women with histories of illness and substance abuse.[8] It affects mothers of special-needs babies disproportionately. PPD was not invented by feminists to shame men; nor was it invented by doctors to further medicalize the processes of birth and mothering. It simply *is*.

Middle-class heterosexual white chicks with PPD—much like your author—get the most press because, I'm ashamed to say, we have the greatest access to healthcare providers, particularly in the United States, where such access is related to our employment and marital status. We have the greatest access to antidepressant medications and psychoanalytic therapy. And it is we who "should" be happy; a deviation from the "happy mother" norm is, in our case, the most glaring. It is less newsworthy when a poor mother, a mother of color, or a single mother is depressed. When people who "have it all" nonetheless lose touch with reality or hurt our children, or ourselves, the outcry is louder.[9]

PPD has been observed and studied in almost every cultural environment imaginable: in rural Uganda, in the United Arab Emirates, among Hmong immigrants, and in northeastern and central Wisconsin.[10]

Middle-class Caucasian women with higher education are also of a culture that values medical intervention and psychoanalytic therapy more highly than do many other cultures. According to Linda Clark Amankwaa, attitudes about postpartum depression and its treatment are affected by culture insofar as different groups possess "a distinctive language related to depression, the transmission of information among people about depression, and beliefs about health care and health care systems."[11]

In a 2000 study of African American women with postpartum depression,

> [p]articipants suggested that depression was something that would not be disclosed readily among African-American people (or outsiders) because of the stigma attached to it and the negative consequences. These negative consequences include past atrocities encountered by African-American people in health care systems, particularly mental health institutional systems where African-American children were taken from their mothers, and other stigmas regarding African-American women's care of their children.[12]

Cultural factors also mitigate a woman's readiness to disclose her postpartum depression. While mental illness is stigmatized almost globally, Rhoda Barge Johnson and Joan Crowley write of a so-called "John Henry" phenomenon, an attitude among some African Americans that hard work—indeed, working oneself to death, like the eponymous folk hero did—is the only way to overcome obstacles.[13] Reaching out for help or admitting weakness carries a greater price.

This certainly does not mean that African American parents do not experience depression. In fact, the converse may well be true: African American parents experience depression as frequently or more often than people of other races, and a crisis of public health policy is afoot.

Employment and migration patterns in North America also complicate the postpartum experience. New parents in the same "newlywed and nearly dead" or commuter neighborhood may never meet; our sisters and mothers may live in different regions. We do not have access to the wisdom of others, except for the "experts"— our pediatricians and childcare gurus—whose prescriptive and impersonal advice undermines our self-confidence.

Researchers theorize that in cultures that practice postpartum ritual and have centralized populations (such as nonindustrialized Africa) "postpartum depression" is less common. According to J. L. Cox, "the lack of obstetric and family rituals lowers a mother's self-esteem, stresses the marital relationship, and can represent an ambivalent social status."[14] In many non-Western cultures a new mother is cared for or attended by a female relation or neighbor for the immediate postpartum period—this is known as "doing the month." Western women receive less social support; indeed, we are expected to "bounce back" on our own within the arbitrary period of six weeks—regaining our prepregnancy figures, resuming "normal" relations with our sexual partners, returning to paid work (if we have it), and shepherding infants who sleep well and are contented. Parenting magazines encourage us to flatten our abdomens, regulate our children's sleeping and eating schedules, dress tastefully, and otherwise *exhibit no signs* of having recently given birth. Our models are soap opera actresses and pop divas with personal trainers and baby nurses, not mothers, sisters, neighbors, or members of our community.

I'm happy to say that with the proliferation of websites and

Internet usergroups devoted to parents with like minds and similar situations, this trend may be reversing itself. I joined a web community for "rebel" mothers (a term loosely defined but encompassing loudmouthed mothers, lesbian mothers, single mothers, artist mothers, combinations of the above, and other maternal nonconformists) and vented my soul to women living in Brazil, Finland, Italy, Canada, and every corner of the United States, from Maine to Hawaii. We traded teething remedies, swapped children's clothes and other necessities (I sent a box of my son's outgrown pajamas to Washington State and got a "sex swing," still in the packaging, in return), and coached each other through complicated pregnancies, divorces, employment and financial crises, addictions and recovery, disastrous haircuts, and cooking with seitan.

There are organized groups for parents of children with autism-spectrum disorders, asthma, celiac disease, and other special needs. There are organized groups for stay-at-home fathers, for widows and widowers, for depressed parents, for mothers of color, for goth parents, for pagan parents, and for innumerable other groups. If a group for you doesn't exist, the technology to start your own is readily available and easily used by nonexperts. This kind of peer-to-peer support was crucial to my own recovery from PPD; I could rant about wanting to leave my fussy, vomiting son on the curb for bulk pickup, and no one judged me.

The Internet also connected me to women in my community; I wouldn't have found them otherwise. One local group offers a volunteer service called "Austin Red Tent," in which a member emails a request for help with a problem and participants mobilize, running errands or bringing chicken soup, Jell-O, meals, or other supplies. I met my playgroup online. I met other depressives. I met family members of suicide victims, and that made a serious fucking impression.

I also learned a hell of a lot: A squirt of breast milk in the eye will heal conjunctivitis. Household vinegar (5 percent acidity) disinfects as well as household bleach. Cloth diapers aren't impossible to use. I learned all kinds of interesting stuff not even related to parenting: I learned how to care for carnivorous plants. I learned about frat-hop music and programming languages. I learned how to help a friend in rehab. I learned about having anal sex safely. (Don't ever, *ever* use that anesthetizing lubricant.) I learned all kinds of neat shit that makes me a better, more informed parent, a happier person, and a good citizen. And I got lots and lots of encouragement, something *all kinds of parents* receive far too infrequently.

Here's another myth about mental illness and PPD in particular: You can just "get over it." In her fine memoir *Sleepless Days*, Susan Kushner Resnick writes that you probably will get better even if you don't do anything, but it will take time. Of course, time is not on the side of a mentally ill person. The cycle for postpartum depression is lengthy. According to the Postpartum Health Alliance, untreated postpartum depression can take three to four years to resolve. That's three to four years of your life, of your kid's life—years you can spend getting crazier, lying awake at night, crying through every day, wishing to die and maybe even trying to, hurting yourself, hurting your kid. (Studies indicate that children of depressive mothers have higher levels of the stress hormone cortisol in their bodies, acquire language with greater difficulty, and are more likely to be psychiatrically disturbed later in life.[15]) There's simply no reason to wait for things to get better.

If any of this sounds like you or someone you love, get help. It will be hard, but living with mental illness is harder. Get ahold of anyone and everyone you can. Tell your neighbor. Tell your doctor if you have one, or your midwife, or your chiropractor. Tell your parents. Tell the person who delivers your mail. Hit the panic button, if that's what it takes. Get your hands on any resource you possibly can. Stop pretending you don't need help, and take any that's offered to you.

It is taboo for mothers to confess their anger, their confusion, their frustration, their resentment. Yet these are feelings we all possess, on our best days and our worst. "Sometimes babies are little sods," a mother from Great Britain told me once. She was a professor at Oxford Brookes University, and from a highly academic twenty-minute discussion of "the moral context in which women continue to mother in the West," this simple truism is my only memory.

So read on. I'll tell you about everything I did. How I went crazy. How I danced around my living room with my fussy kid to inappropriate music. How my marriage hit the skids. How I survived therapy, six doctors, and a naturopath. How I went out to kill myself but couldn't get a baby sitter. And how I got my shit together and went on with my life somehow. I'm not telling you what to do, exactly—perhaps my life is not like yours, or perhaps I benefited from resources to which you have no access, or perhaps you simply went crazy differently, or not quite at all—but I will tell you what I did. By sharing our voices, perhaps we will all feel less alone. For the worst thing about my year of madness was how alone I felt, locked in solitary battle with voices in my head that told me I was a shameful and malignant being in a world of maternal benevolence and perfection. If I had listened carefully, I would have heard the desperation other mothers expressed to me quietly. Looking back now, from a place of relative sanity, I see maternal anger everywhere, bubbling through the veneer of politesse, reaching out from inside the platitudinous language we turn to when we are confounded: "I thought I was going to lose my mind." Yet in my own moments of derangement, I needed to be taken by the hand and shown. I needed a voice as loud as my own internal monologue of self-hate. As a writer, I possess a loud voice. And I intend to speak my peace with it if you'd care to listen.

DREAD

MOTHER'S DAY IS ONE of those pastel wrist-corsage holidays. In the kindest scenario, we pack Mom in the Buick and take her to Sunday buffet. She gets a card with roses and glitter script. We thank her for her unflinching support all those years as we attempted field hockey and the autoharp.

But motherhood—at least as I've experienced it—is the kind of hair-raising experience that calls for a more primal celebration, perhaps with burning herbs, bread baked in the shape of babies, and keening. Behind Mom's beatific smile is a nest of emotions, from purest joy to total heartbreak.

If there is a definitive statement on the heartbreak of parenthood, it might be *Decalogue: One*, the first in a series of shorts directed by Polish filmmaker Krzysztof Kieslowski. The story is about a mathematician and his precocious son. The two delight in science—calculating, predicting, and quantifying—and the boy, Pawel, wants to know when their neighborhood pond will be fully frozen for skating. They conclude one morning that the pond is safe: The ground temperature has been below freezing for many days. They are unaware that the crew of a nearby power station has released hot water into the pond overnight.

As mothers, we plan for every exigency. So does Pawel's father.

And we offer tender gestures when we fail—just as Pawel's aunt zips up his jacket before his body is rolled away to the morgue on a stretcher. We know that our displays of care are ultimately futile. We are powerless against a world of horrors: iatrogenic errors, blood-borne viruses, careless or intoxicated motorists, terrorist actions, septicemia, neoplasms of uncertain behavior and of unspecified nature. When I was eleven, I watched as the last of these maladies killed my sister, two years older. It grew silently inside her brain until she just stopped breathing one day. I watched my parents flail for an answer, as the mathematician does after Pawel drowns. Well-intentioned neighbors brought roast and pie; they lit candles in their respective places of worship. But the lesson of the story, and of Kieslowski's, is that ours is a world of chaos. We give it meaning only by our attempts to mitigate one another's suffering. We cannot make the mistake of pride, of trusting that science or reason or ideology can allow us to surmount the ineffable.

These thoughts whirled in my head while I was pregnant. I'd spend night after night lying on the couch, unable to lay to rest my questions about the little feet that kicked inside me. We were unsafe at every moment. I wore myself out hammering cabinet locks into place, researching the dangers of heavy metals in fish, fretting about the Moscow Mules and Xanax I'd had before I realized I was going to have a baby. Were routine sonograms dangerous? Should we vaccinate? Were my outlets overloaded? If my air bag deployed accidentally, would the force crush the fetus? Was I oligohydramniotic?

Consequently, I was not a jolly pregnant lady. I did not eat

Twinkies and knit. I was surly and sleep deprived. I had hollows under my eyes. I was profane and flatulent. At work I kept my office door closed and my headphones on. No one objected. The rest of the time I skulked around in sweatpants, glaring at people. I knew things I couldn't handle were in store.

Other people didn't seem to have this problem. I endured a horrific childbirth preparation class with expectant couples bubbling over with glee, talking about their nursery furnishings and gift showers. Periodically, a husband would liken the childbirth experience to some form of discomfort he experienced routinely—lifting weights or dislocating a trick shoulder. We played icebreaker games and watched *Bill Cosby, Himself.* I wanted to throw myself out the window.

I had one moment of happiness during my pregnancy: the day I found out. I went out into the living room with the test stick and rifled through our music collection in search of something suitable for the occasion.

"You're going to like this," I told my stomach. "There are really beautiful things out here in the world, and this music is one of them."

I put on Elliott Smith's *XO*, which is one of my favorite albums. I sat down on the floor by the speakers and felt around on my abdomen. I listened very closely until it was over, hearing statements like, "I wish I'd never seen your face," and "The doctor orders drinks all night to take away this curse."

It's not *Up with People.* But it's true and comforting; it says something real, like *Decalogue: One.* It mitigated my suffering when I was sad. It meant something. And it contains the one wisdom every parent needs to communicate to a child over the course of his or her lifetime: *Everybody knows you only live a day. But it's brilliant anyway.*

Of course, Elliott Smith would be dead from an apparently self-inflicted stab wound before my son's second birthday.

DEPRESSION IS UGLY

I DON'T KNOW WHY ANYONE THINKS depression is romantic. I guess technically the Romantics had it. (By that I mean Shelley and Keats and Coleridge and all, not the 1980s pop band—though who knows how they're feeling these days?) I guess we have these images of tormented loners weeping on moors or whatnot. I feel more like Stuart Smalley, Al Franken's badly sweatered *Saturday Night Live* therapy cliché. Spare me the Laudanum; I'm more likely to medicate myself with Benadryl and half a Dutch apple pie.

I moved all my black clothes to the bottom drawer when my son started projectile-vomiting breast milk on them, and my lipstick (Urban Decay's Roach) doesn't stay put after compulsive eating, so maybe the problem is me. Maybe I'm not attractive enough to be a Tragic Melancholic, or a Wise Fool, or a Free-Spirited Flake on the Run from Herself, or whatever the hell sexy depressives are. I'm more like Schlumpfy Hausfrau in Sweatpants on Paxil, and nobody wants to be that person.

I tried to be a sexy depressive when I was younger. It didn't work. I tried to write poetry for the lit mag. I have no ability with meter. I smoked cloves, but it was too inconvenient to buy them at head shops, and once, in a fit of postadolescent pique, I locked myself in my bedroom and listened to The Smiths' "Girl Afraid" on repeat. I lasted about twenty minutes, and then I had to come out to use the bathroom, and no one had noticed that I was missing.

I was even less successful as a political depressive. Political depressives are really hot stuff. I love this argument, the "shouldn't we all be crazy when the world is insane?" bit, the *One Flew Over the Cuckoo's Nest* version of mental illness. One of my heroes, Ariel Gore, advances this opinion in an essay entitled "60 Tablets of Wellbutrin (May Cause Drowsiness)": "No use changing the world, after all, when we can just change everyone's brain chemistry." She also warns, "One side effect is that [antidepressants] can make you politically cooperative." Maybe this is a risk if you're really truly fighting The Man, and I get how people get worn down from shit jobs, shit relationships, shit housing, shit air, shit water, prepackaged blobs of frozen shit food, shit government, shit lives, shit brains, shit hearts, shit in our blood, blood in our shit, shit drugs, shit in our lungs. Isn't it logical to be depressed? Verily. Isn't it better for us to "feel our feelings," as I've so often heard, instead of blunting them with pharmaceuticals? Sure.

But it didn't work for me. I'd still be slumped over in the corner. So I called my obstetrician and made an appointment. When I arrived, I was actually wearing pants and shoes; it felt strange. I sat in a straight-backed chair in a tasteful pink examining room with back issues of *Woman's Day* in a Lucite keeper, and I told the nurse the deal. I was depressed. I was humiliated. I couldn't stop crying. I couldn't get the baby to stop crying. I was a horrible parent. I couldn't sleep. I'd be listening for any sound I could hear. I'd hear my eyelids open and close. I'd get disoriented. I once stood on the top floor of the library looking for the 600s, at the north of the building. Which way was north? What direction was I facing? Where was the river?

I'd sometimes have to put the baby down in the bassinet screaming, and I'd walk to the front of the house and close a door and yell every obscenity I could think of and dig my nails into my arms. And there was the cutting and the things I wanted to do to myself. It never stopped. There was never a good day. There was never a different day. It went minute by minute. I was up all day and up all night. I couldn't make it stop. It would never stop.

I tried to be very precise in explaining my symptoms, evincing that I had the presence of mind to understand my situation. I was intelligent and concise and used terms like "suicidal ideation" to prove that I was a good patient. I wasn't psychotic. I didn't see things or hear things that weren't there. But I had thoughts that surprised me, which had never happened before, when I had generated all my own thoughts consciously for myself. Now it was like a surprise party was going on in my brain. I was meeting new people in there. Was that a problem?

The doctor and I talked about the baby. The nurse hugged me. "We've all been there," she said. Why is there a special term for it? Why do we describe this experience as if it were unusual?

"Is motherhood just like this?" I asked my mother. My mother is the most even-keeled, Girl Scout troop–leading, van-driving soccer mom in the universe.

"Sure. I think it's like this for everybody," she said.

"Did you hate me? Did you want to die?" I asked.

"Oh, honey," she told me. "I used to sit in the rocking chair and just cry and cry."

So I started taking Zoloft, which made me feel like a plucked string. I can remember literally pogoing up and down in my pullman-style kitchen, keenly aware of every blue swirl in the tile on the floor. Jim and my mother looked on with concern.

"You feel zingy?" my doctor asked. "Okay, let's see if that stops and levels off."

It did. Then I was taking a blue prescription M&M in the morning. Nothing.

I wrote:

> I hate this child. Becoming a mother was the worst fucking mistake I ever made. I want to put this kid in a fucking tree, send him off with the carnival. Everything I've ever done for this fucking kid hasn't been enough. I want my fucking life back. I want to be able to take a shower and have a job. I want to be able to make a sandwich without somebody hanging on my legs screaming at me. You could give me electroshock and Thorazine but not a fucking thing is going to change until my kid starts acting like a fourteen-month-old instead of a colicky infant.

I saw a therapist who had framed pictures of her dog. She tried to talk me out of my depression by confusing me further.

"I feel completely miserable in every moment. I'm miserable now," I told her.

"I see. Well, you're in a bad situation. Why wouldn't you be miserable?" she said.

I didn't get it.

"Wouldn't anyone in your situation be miserable? Why do you think you should be happy? Let's talk about your expectations."

"So I should accept being miserable? Isn't that the opposite of therapy?"

"Well, I think we'll start by making a list of all your 'shoulds.' You 'should' be happy. You 'should' want to have sex. Why do you have these expectations?"

"Aren't people supposed to want to be happy? So we go to therapy for that purpose?" I wasn't clear on what we were trying to accomplish.

"What do you think would make you happy?"

I hesitated. I thought about it. I wanted ice cream.

"So stop and get some ice cream on your way home! Do some special things for yourself."

The Zoloft went up to 100 milligrams. New doctor.

I caused this person, this baby, to exist. I couldn't kill him, I didn't want to hurt him, I didn't have Mr. Peabody and the Wayback Machine, so I couldn't stop myself from having conceived. What could I do? There was nothing. I was stuck. What if I left, just left?

I had a panic attack while driving down the freeway. I made myself breathe out of my mouth until I could take the next exit, find a gas station, call my mother, get her to talk me down.

The holidays came. I wrote:

All I ever do is BABY BABY BABY and I'm going to get all Courtney Love crazy on the first one of my idiot relatives who makes some dumb-ass comment about how the baby "should" be sleeping and I "should" be getting back to work because, fuck, it's just not happening. I'm not sending any Christmas cards (sorry, all y'all that sent them to me) and I'm not cooking and I'm not doing any editing work and I haven't had sex in months and I don't even have time to go to therapy because the Perpetual Crying Machine that is my child can't be without me for ten minutes. It's a glorious fucking day if I get Zoloft in my mouth and pants on my ass. Everyone will receive their holiday gifts via the "close your eyes and hold out your hands" method, and we will truly be the jolliest bunch of assholes this side of the nut house.

"I don't think Paxil will be different," my doctor said. "It's in the same class of drugs. You should consider weaning."

Thirty tablets of Paxil, 37.5 milligrams. I insisted.

I wrote:

I am a shitty parent. I resent my kid and wish he wasn't born. I have to hold him tightly in my arms to immobilize him before naptime. After almost an hour of trying to get him back to sleep just now, I finally dumped him on the bed (a little roughly, I'm afraid) and ran out of the room crying. Let Jim handle it. Of course Jim isn't able to get the baby to sleep at all. He wants mama, mama, mama, mama. I hear the baby crying right now, through my earplugs.

See what I mean? How sexy is this shit? Not very. Nor could I be accused of not feeling my feelings. I was fucking feeling my feelings, all right.

My mom sighed. "I think it's just going to be like this for you."

"For how long?"

First they'd said colic would last three months. Then they said reflux would last eight months. Then they said the eczema would last two years, if we were lucky. There was some evidence that kids could outgrow peanut allergy, or that a new experimental therapy could lessen the likelihood of anaphylactic shock.

"Until he's in school."

"You're kidding."

"Don't have another one."

I tried the *Lysistrata* technique. No more sex until Jim has a vasectomy. He shrugged. We weren't having sex anyway.

I kept taking the Paxil. I started writing and here I am. I woke up to a rash and a screaming kid this morning at 3:30. It's more manageable most days. You could say it's better.

I sure wish I could be sexy or political, though. I wish depressive mothers could have alt.fan Usenet groups. I wish people would write graphic novels about depressive maternal superheroes who manage to get out of bed and floss and resist suicide. I want to have wannabes sporting my Look, the barfed-on, yogurt-crusted bra tank, the baggy shorts, the Chapstick and bare feet and mosquito bites and orange-juice breath. I wish people would write fanfic about me: *When I get to the house, Marrit opens the door in a bathrobe of ratty pink chenille. She is finishing off a lemon pie and listening to Ministry. I have her Paxil and egg-free doughnuts. I see her eyes flash and her lips part slightly, gratitude flowing from her skin as she takes my hand.*

LUBRICATING MY CHILD

YOU NAME IT, I'VE APPLIED IT to my child. Okay, so I never bathed him in the blood of virgins, and I haven't yet smeared him with yak fat, but nothing is out of the question.

If you, your kid, or someone else you like has eczema or psoriasis, you probably know what I'm talking about: Funky rashes. Flaky skin. Weeping sores. Staph infections. And the ever-popular *scaling*. Yes, nothing says "sexy" like eczema.

Most kids have cradle cap, and Baldo was no exception. He'd scratch and scratch, even in his sleep. We'd scrub it with the little brush from the hospital, the thing that looks like a potato washer. Then he developed what I could only describe as "eyebrow cap." I was reluctant to scrub his face like a yam.

"That's dermatitis," the first pediatrician said. "Put some over-the-counter cortisone cream on it."

We did. I'd have to hold Baldo's screaming head in both my hands while somehow squeezing out a pea-size dab of Cortaid. Good thing I have that third hand.

It seemed helpful at first. His big red eyebrows, which gave him an expression of perpetual surprise, returned to the blondish wisps of yore, much like my skimpy eyebrows, which make me look kind of like a burn victim. Then along came the discoid eczema, the scaly round patches I recognized from the arms of my husband. "It's eczema!" I cackled. At last, someone to blame. "You did this to us!"

Thus we began moisturizing furiously. I sought advice from the mothers I know, online and in real life. In came the recommendations. Calendula cream. Florasone, a homeopathic treatment made of *Cardiospermum*, a "flowering vine that has been used as a medicine in India and Africa for centuries," read the label. Plain old Johnson & Johnson baby lotion. A treatment, popularized in Japan, that involved sitting in a pond while tiny fish ate the eczema off the sufferer's skin. We attempted all but the last, and though we found most success with the baby lotion, it left the baby's skin feeling slightly tacky, as if we'd applied some of that mysterious gel file clerks apply to their fingertips before rifling through a big stack of papers.

"I don't like this at all," the first pediatrician said. "I don't like the rash with the reflux."

"It's eczema, we're sure," I piped up. "It looks just like his father's. See?" I pointed to Jim's arm.

The doctor rubbed the baby's leg. "See how his skin feels waxy? I don't like this at all."

We scowled and said nothing.

We put flaxseed oil in Baldo's oatmeal. We bathed him less frequently. We bathed him more frequently. We stopped using soap. We stopped using shampoo. We put baby oil on his head. We put olive oil in his bath. We put olive oil on his head.

"Let me get this straight," Aunt Erin marveled. "You *season* your child? Like a skillet?"

"Like a Thanksgiving turkey," we said.

Back to the pediatrician's office we went. We came home with Triamcinolone, our first prescription-strength steroid. "It's well within the safe range," the doctor reassured us.

I put the Triamcinolone on the top shelf of our pantry with the household bleach, ant baits, and other hazardous materials and resumed lotioning furiously. I was afraid—afraid of thinning the baby's skin, afraid of suppressing his immune system, afraid of stunting his growth. He'd grow up to be a cigar-smoking homunculus, like Baby Huey.

"Have you seen this insert?" I waved the box around. *Plastic pants or tight-fitting diapers may increase the chance of absorption of the medicine through the skin and the chance of side effects.* Numbness in fingers? Pus-containing blisters in hair follicles? Unusual increase in hair growth? Weakness of the arms?

Just the same, the eczema didn't respond. "The baby's reacting to something in your breast milk," the doctor said. "Have you cut out dairy?"

Out went the milk proteins. After a month, nothing. Out went the soy. Nothing. Thus began the elimination diet. I'd wake up to a glass of pear juice and a big bowl of brown rice. I went to the natural-foods supermarket and bought organic brown-rice versions of everything: pasta, milk, crackers, cakes, brown rice made from brown rice. I fantasized about forbidden wheat flour. I dreamed once that I was lying atop a giant buttermilk pancake, being absorbed into its delicate papery honeycombs. I was turning into real creamery butter. Still nothing helped.

Then it was time for the hypoallergenic predigested baby formula from England. It cost $45 a can, was only available through the pharmacy, and smelled like rancid chicken soup. It was full of corn-syrup solids and synthetic amino acids. It came in giant cans and required boiled water, so we'd whip up a big batch for the day every morning. None of this fancy-pants, ready-to-feed stuff. No single-serving packets. I'd have to somehow schlep refrigerated Neocate wherever we went. And after a promising first day, the shit started coming back up on us. Barfed, it smelled even worse, while Baldo's shit was mysteriously dense and black. Neither liquid nor solid, it was its own state of matter. I put Baldo back on the boob.

"I'm going to tell you something that might make you say goodbye to me and find another pediatrician," the doctor warned. "You're too invested in breastfeeding."

Was I? We were putting ourselves through an awful lot of contortions. But what was the alternative?

"You know," he added. "Children's gastrointestinal disorders can be so tragic. Like celiac disease. And cancer."

Cancer?

"Yeah."

"Are you saying I'm going to give my son cancer by nursing him?"

"No, no. It's just that we really need to take this seriously."

We took it so seriously that our next stop was the children's hospital for a consult. First came an ultrasound to determine if reflux was present.

"Oh, it's present," I told the technician.

"Well, we'll just watch what happens." We needed to see if there was an obstruction in Baldo's gastrointestinal tract, what they call pyloric stenosis. It can require surgery.

A nurse produced a bottle of barium solution for Baldo.

"He's not gonna drink that." I was aghast. The nipple was all wrong, some brown rubber Playtex something-or-other that was shaped like my nipple might have been if somebody clamped it and ran halfway across the room. My son hated bottles. Surely he would hate a bottle of barium.

He pounded it and burped.

"Okay, that's good," the doctor said. "Now let's just have you hold him flat against the table on his back, Mom, and we'll take a look." I hate it when people other than my child call me "Mom." It's so Operation Rescue.

There we stood in our lead aprons, waiting. Nothing unusual appeared on the screen. Baldo's gizzards pumped and processed the glowing swill.

"I don't see anything out of the ordinary," the doctor said, and she began turning away to scribble in her chart. *Pow!* Up came a tide of white, chalky vomit. It splattered me, it splattered the nurse, it splattered my mom, who was along to watch and help. It was the single most brilliant instance of reverse peristalsis I had ever witnessed in my life. It was in my hair.

"It's reflux," the doctor reassessed. Somebody produced an extra-large package of baby wipes, and we began cleaning up.

On our way out, she took me aside. "You're still nursing, right?" I nodded, and she continued, "Keep on doing it. Too many doctors tell the mother something's wrong with her milk, when it's actually the best thing for it."

"I didn't nurse her," my mother interjected, cocking her head in my direction. My mom volunteers this information, I think, in a kind of *auto-da-fé* whenever anyone extols the benefits of breast-feeding. But it was the 1970s when I was a baby. Formula feeding was supposed to be the Great Liberator. That's just how it was. No hard feelings.

On to the pediatric gastroenterologist. We waited in a common room used by all the pediatric specialists for their patients, including the oncologists. It was sobering.

"It's stupid for us to be here," I whispered to Jim. "It's just reflux. These other kids are really sick."

We waited and waited. I joggled Baldo in the Björn while he nursed and cried, cried, cried. Finally even the kids with cancer were staring at us. Maybe it wasn't stupid, exactly, but still the pendulum swung: (1) We are ridiculous, pampered Westerners who panic just because our baby cries a little and subject him to torturous medical interventions, and (2) We are going to lose our minds if this baby cries for another minute.

The gastroenterologist drew a diagram of Baldo's digestive tract on a dry-erase board and pointed to the hinky parts. He'll grow out of it, she assured us. She told us he was gaining weight well enough. There was no cause for alarm. There was no need for the "string test," which measures the amount of digestive acid regurgitated by the baby and requires an overnight hospital stay. We should continue nursing. She even wrote "continue nursing" on the form that would go back to our pediatrician. I read it and reread it all the way home. We decided our pediatrician was a massive ass clown and could go fuck himself.

The second pediatrician gave us a prescription for Elidel, a non-steroidal cream that had tested promisingly. Nothing. Onward to Elocon, an even stronger corticosteroid cream, and our first prescription antihistamine, which we'd administer at night with an oral syringe.

"That'll make him sleepy," the pharmacist claimed. We laughed ruefully. Yeah, right.

We celebrated Baldo's first birthday with a wheat-free yellow cake. The recipe called for xanthan gum, which cost $12 for a tiny bag. I don't know how people manage this shit—$12 for a weird bag of God-knows-what that makes a thing like a big, caramel-frosted hockey puck. I was carving the cake up when a couple poked their heads into the kitchen where my friend Andrea was hosting the party.

"Is there really a wheat-free cake in here?" They were wide eyed.

"It's this one." I pointed to it. It was lopsided and collapsing. The dad turned back to the living room and hollered, "C'mere, honey, there's a cake you can eat!"

A little blond girl, probably five or six years old, materialized in the doorway. We cut her a piece of cake and she ran off with it. It turned out she had celiac disease and couldn't eat gluten. I wasn't even entirely sure what gluten was, but I knew my cake had none, except maybe in the vanilla, and the parents told me not to worry about that.

"She never gets to eat cake at parties," the mother explained. "Sometimes we bring a snack for her, but she always wants what the other kids have."

I grinned all the way home, even when Baldo barfed in his car seat. We had to pull over in the parking lot of a high school. It was a Sunday night, but the lot was full of cars, discharging fresh-scrubbed kids in Dockers and dresses who were carrying band instruments into the auditorium for a recital. Some of them lingered to observe our puke-soaked, squalling infant. I had to wipe up the barf with our baby sling.

"This really does sound like a food sensitivity," the second pediatrician declared.

Apparently, there's a whole weird world of allergic people. I'm not one of them. They wear ear tubes and carry steroid inhalers and shrink from pollen-producing plants. They go to chiropractors and homeopaths and take herbal tinctures. They sleep on funky pillows, rip up carpeting, and wrap their mattresses in specially designed expensive plastic thingies. Jim's half of the medicine cabinet is full of antihistamines and nasal sprays with futuristic-looking plungers. They have names like "Alanose" and "Nasorol." I'm not allergic to anything, except for penicillin and sulfa drugs, so I am only beginning to develop sympathy for these people. East Texans practically dunk their children in giant vats of pine pollen and wrap them in cat pelts, then feed them chipotle peppers and surround them with ruminant farm animals. Naturally, I thought allergies afflicted candy-pants Californians and sympathy-cravers, kids whose overbearing mothers always described them as "delicate" and wouldn't let them participate in PE. Boy, was I getting schooled.

At the allergist's office, I ran into one of my old coworkers. "For him?" she pointed to Baldo, incredulous. "Already?"

My coworker, it turns out, is one of these allergic people. "I am waiting for my shots," she said. She is a native speaker of Portuguese and uses very few contractions. "It is no fun to have these allergies."

"He's probably just going to be an allergy kid," the doctor agreed. "You'll be lucky if he stops here and doesn't develop asthma." With his hands, the doctor demonstrated the "allergy march," a progression from eczema to allergies to asthma. With my hands, I tried to keep Baldo from scratching his fingers raw. There was an oogy spot on the webby part between one thumb and forefinger. It was turning green.

We left with another steroid cream, Locoid, and another antihistamine, Zyrtec. We were instructed to return after the RAST tests were completed. It turned out that the baby was allergic to three things: eggs, cats, and peanuts. I remembered the three eggs *and* mayonnaise that went into the gluten-free cake and almost slapped myself. I slapped myself again upon recalling the days and nights of the elimination diet, conducted while Scooter, the family tabby, curled his body around Baldo like a feline question mark. I slapped myself a third time upon recalling the metric assloads of peanut butter I shoveled in while I was pregnant, even though I knew better, and the Reese's peanut butter cup I absentmindedly ate on Halloween. I adore peanut butter. It's nasty and wicked. You can spread it on anything: chocolate, your lover, a lawnmower. It's also fatal for some people, like our friend Kevin's ex-girlfriend, Wendy, who'd make him brush his teeth before he could even talk to her after a peanut butter milkshake from Mr. Frosty. And that kid at Jim's school, who was so allergic that he had to be sequestered in a special room during testing, lest some other pupil produce a peanut butter cracker from his backpack and introduce peanut *dust* into the room.

"Fuck. Fuck. Fuck," I told the pharmacist. When you fill a prescription for an Epi-Pen—the shot of concentrated antihistamine you administer to avoid anaphylactic shock after an accidental exposure—the pharmacy staff actually pulls their fingers out of their butts and rallies like a team of medics.

"We'll get this filled right away!" cried the goateed tech for whom I usually have to spell and re-spell my last name, pointing at the seldom-used bin for the letter I.

The egg-elimination diet is a big pain in the ass. As I type this, I'm still on it. People put eggs in the most unnecessary places. Don't brush that shit on a pie crust to make it glossy. Don't put it in your goddamn burgers. Just leave it out. Don't put it in doughnuts. Don't put it in ice cream. I can't eat anything except goddamn vanilla. Everything I love has eggs in it, except for my son.

Finally the dermatologist met with us. He gave us a new tacrolimus cream called Protopic.

"Is that approved for children under two?" I challenged.

He shrugged. "No, but we still use it."

"Just curious." By now I didn't care if it was made from the urine of pregnant mares and tested on Marines.

It turns out I liked the Protopic so much that I composed in my head *Protopic: The Musical.* Grateful eczema sufferers would dance and sing, waving their boar-bristled toothbrushes and all-cotton socks. It helps a lot.

We still lubricate Baldo twice a day with bovine udder cream. We still bathe him without soap. We still wash his clothes in hypoallergenic detergent. We still give him antihistamines at night to help him sleep. We still keep shoes on him at all times during the day and dress him in footed pajamas year round. His thumbs still look oogy from time to time. And sometimes he does break out fully; then we break out the steroids.

And if indeed he does turn out to be a wheezing, feeble child, like Piggy in *Lord of the Flies,* we can only hope he'll become a master persuader, a boy of noble strength and silver tongue. I don't want the other children to use him as a protein source.

ARE YOU **OKAY?**

THE FIRST PERSON I ASKED was sitting two seats away from us at the Baby Matinee. She looked kind of like me, in fact: short red hair, little black glasses, acrylic cardigan sweater. There was one significant difference: The baby she was holding was sleeping and not rashy, and the mother wasn't blubbering hysterically.

We'd gotten better by this point. The reflux had stopped recently. The Paxil had kicked in. I was cocky enough that I'd taken it upon myself to scout around. How could no one notice the thousands of crazy bitches running around with babies until we flipped out and did something desperate and psychotic? Surely my PPD detector would trip in the presence of others—too many pies in the checkout line, the little nervous squiggle of a hysterical half-smile, a whiff of maternal flop sweat. I could strap a utility belt over my BREEDER t-shirt, load myself down with calming floral tinctures, Luna Bars, paperback copies of *The Mask of Motherhood*, some of those free movie passes I was always getting in the mail. Maybe I'd have a little tin of salon texturizer, a cell phone with endless minutes for panicked calls to psychotherapists, a Pez dispenser full of Xanax. I'd race around town in the Volvotron 3000 with Jerry Reed's "East Bound and Down" as my theme song, intercepting panicked parents at pediatrician's offices and playgroups.

"I'll watch the baby! You guys go get lunch by yourselves!"

"But . . . but . . . how can we ever repay you, Badass Survivor Woman?"

"Never mind that! Your mental health is my reward!"

As usual, it didn't work out that way.

People don't like it when you inquire about their mental health, especially if you're some strange person next to them at the movies.

"Say, that's a small baby you have there. How old is your little one?"

"Thirteen weeks." The mother smiled hesitantly.

I paused. "Is everything going all right?"

"Oh, yeah." She nodded politely, then resumed staring at the screen. The theater we frequent plays wacky film loops without sound before the house lights go down and the previews start rolling.

"And is everything okay with you?"

She turned back to me and didn't respond immediately.

I raised my eyebrows. "I mean, the newborn stage is really tough. Are you feeling all right?"

"Oh . . . sure." She smiled indulgently. End of conversation.

I could have pushed it: *You took a long time to answer. Are you sure you're not depressed? Do you sleep when the baby sleeps? Do you feel sufficiently supported by your loved ones? Have you had any panic attacks? Thoughts of hurting yourself? Have you lost interest in the activities you usually enjoy? Have these feelings persisted for two weeks or longer?*

You can't ask these questions.

*

What was she going to say? No, no, no, yes, yes, yes, yes? And then I was going to give her a hug and be her PPD pledge sister? Decorate her front door with paper cutouts and stickers? Take her out for ice cream?

You'd have better luck with this: *So, how much weight have you lost? Is your episiotomy healed? Does your pussy still feel like ground chuck? Did you fail at breastfeeding? Is your house a total shitpit?*

I'd discovered from my own experience socializing with other mothers that we could talk about just about anything other than mental illness. We could eat braised puppy and defecate on each other before the topic of PPD would come up. I knew this. But I thought everything would be different, now that I wasn't the crazy one. My benevolence would inspire other people to open up instantly, to revel in my warmth and generosity. And truthfully, I have difficulty socializing with other women, aside from Baldo's "Aunt" Erin, who works because she's as awkward and standoffish as I am. I lost my sister, and I always wanted her back in surrogate form, but how do you ask for that?

The second time I asked, we were in the pediatrician's office for Baldo's eighteen-month checkup. Baldo was ripping around the waiting room in unusually high spirits, while others in the room were catatonic on some Disney movie playing on a video monitor. (I hate that the office does that instead of offering enough toys for all the kids.) It's a large clinic with several physicians and nurse practitioners, so there's always a crowd. In one corner I noticed a couple with a days-old newbie in a baby bucket on the floor between them. In her hands the mother held a breastfeeding diary covered in scrawl. They were gazing down at the industrial carpet with expressionless faces.

I lay in wait until Baldo's capering caught their attention; then I sidled up next to them and projected fellow-parent kindliness at maximum volume. The father watched Baldo hunker down at the kid-size drawing table.

"Wow, he's checking out everything," he observed. "He's not interested in the TV at all."

"We don't watch TV at home," I noted. This was true. It was the one expectation I had while pregnant that we were able to meet. In fact, I couldn't interest Baldo in the television, not even when I had a horribly explosive rotavirus, or when I was prone on the floor with acute hepatitis and would have given anything for a chance to close my eyes and make the room stop spinning.

The dad beamed. "He's going to be really smart."

I shrugged. "Say, that's a little one you have there."

The mom looked up. "Two-week checkup."

"Wow," I said. "Is everything going okay?"

They looked at each other. "We're still tired," the mom admitted. "But the baby's great."

"Fantastic." This was a dead end. I sat down and watched Baldo amuse himself at the table. I felt gratified in many ways; my kid was playing independently for, like, the first time *ever*, and a stranger had, in essence, correlated my parenting to my son's future intelligence. Wasn't this a *Parents* magazine wet dream, aside from the ithcing, weeping trash?

Then I noticed another couple with a two-week-old sitting on the other side of me. Both silent. Dressed in professional-looking officewear, maybe mid-thirties? The kind of parents I don't normally approach because I feel like a weird, overgrown kid with green glitter nail polish and zits when I stand next to them. I just watched them furtively and sensed that something was wrong. I don't even know what it was, or why, or what I wanted to say, but we all sat there in the room with *Lady and the Tramp* on the screen until the nurse called them and they picked up the "baby bucket" and carried the baby out of the room without saying anything.

Maybe I was mistaken. I thought about them the whole time the doctor was poking Baldo and peering into his ears. And when a baby started to cry, probably after getting a shot, I thought about them again, because that baby cried and cried and wouldn't quiet down afterward. I heard that baby crying as Baldo and I walked hand in hand to the door and I hefted him up into my arms and carried him back to the car.

The last time I asked was at a playgroup in our local anarchist bookstore collective. The host is a casual friend of ours, and she has a pranksterish, elfin daughter a few months younger than Baldo is. The mom has different hair every time I see her, and she and her husband took the baby on a national tour with their punk band while I was still bouncing Baldo in circles around the living room with vomit on my shirt. She makes pins that say PUNK PARENT and ROCKER MOM; I fastened one to my diaper bag, even though I'm neither of the above. Anyhow, I figured if I were going to say something provocative or unsettling, these people could probably handle it, with their bumper stickers that say FUCK AUTHORITY and NOBODY FOR PRESIDENT.

The downside is that anarchist playgroups are, as you might expect, largely free from rules imposed upon others. This is fine until my kid gets ahold of something dangerously allergenic that's been stuffed into the hollows of the couch and I have to wrest it from his indignant grasp. I have become The Man.

A lovely, youngish-seeming mother arrived late in the day with her twelve-week-old son snuggled into a particularly cute and utilitarian sling, which we all cooed over and coveted. Her own mother was with her; she was one of those sassy, silver-haired spitfire Texan ladies, like Molly Ivins and Ann Richards. They blended seamlessly into the group, although it was their first visit. The mother breastfed effortlessly while the grandmother chatted up the volunteer at the register and perused the zine rack. Finally, there was a quiet moment when the new mother and I were more or less alone in the play area; the other toddlers had upended a coffee pot placed on a low shelf, and there was much frantic mopping.

"How are you doing?" I asked. Then, because that's such a meaningless conversation starter, I added, "Really."

I watched her face transform—from what to what, I wasn't sure. "I'm doing just fine," she asserted.

(Later, as I sat stupidly and listened to a conversation among the group, I realized that she was a teenage single mother whose babydaddy had declined to be on the birth certificate and is basically a louse. Her extended family members are freaky fundamentalists who've rejected her for having sex before marriage. My question seems to have undermined her. But how could I have known? Should I have known? Shouldn't I have considered the possibility?)

"I'm really glad things are going well," I said, backpedaling. Was it time for a candid admission? I kept babbling.

"'Cause, you know, I was a complete nutcase for pretty much the whole first year," I added, grinning like an idiot.

Then she just looked alarmed, like I was going to grab her baby and eat him.

"It's just so hard being a mother," I concluded. It was my turn to stare at the floor.

I said goodbye when playgroup was over and went home. No resolution.

In a turn of events that could happen only in Austin, that same young mother materialized at the door one day, about a year later. Not my door, but Erin's. Erin had been admitted to rehab in California, and I was house-sitting for her. I'd taken a few hours off from Baldo one weekend morning so I could watch *Red Cockroaches*, an experimental digital-video movie about sibling incest and alienation in a postapocalyptic New York City. I was reviewing *Red Cockroaches* for the Cine Las Americas film festival. So it was already kind of a strange day.

"I'm her neighbor." She hooked her thumb in the direction of the bungalow across the street. "We haven't seen Erin in a while. Is everything okay?"

Everything was getting to be okay, I said. Everything was closer to okay than it had been before. I hadn't realized the extent of Erin's alcoholism until she called me from Palm Desert to tell me that during the worst day of Baldo's infancy, when she and I took turns pacing the floor with him screaming in the sling and crying our eyes out into the couch, she had been having a massive blackout. She'd given me a rousing pep talk the likes of which I'd never heard; it was Vince Lombardi and Alexander Nevsky combined. It was a major turning point in my motherhood. And she remembers none of it.

"Well," said Erin's neighbor, "I'm glad to hear that she's going to be okay."

We looked at each other for a few moments. Then she walked back to the bungalow across the street, and I resumed *Red Cockroaches*.

"My neighbor says she knows you," Erin told me later, when she got home. She came back from California with her hair bleached blond, and she was chain-smoking and talking in acronyms from group. "She says she met you at that anarchist bookstore."

Oh, shit. I hadn't been quite able to place her.

I finally got to apologize one afternoon as we exchanged pleasantries outside Erin's house.

"The first time we met, I'm afraid I said something that must have offended you horribly," I admitted, "and I'm really sorry."

"You were the only person to really ask," she said after a while. "Thanks."

HEPATITIS

MY FIRST VACATION AWAY FROM BALDO began when I developed hepatitis. It started innocuously enough, when I had been fighting off a sinus infection for two weeks. It was April 2003.

"Go to the doctor," Sheila, my mom, commanded. Back I went to the same Hawaiian-shirted osteopath from whom I'd had to pry my prescription for Paxil. Managed care and all.

I don't know why doctors are skeptical of patients claiming to have secondary infections. It's not as if there's a street trade in antibiotics. Is there? What is this, *The Third Man?*

"It's a sinus infection, I'm pretty sure," I said.

"A week, you've had it?"

"Fifteen days."

"Open." He looked into my throat. "Your sputum, is it clear?"

"No." I hate the word "sputum."

"Well, what color is it?"

"It's, uh, foamy and yellow."

The doctor made a face. "Okay, it says on your chart that you're allergic to penicillin. What happens?"

"I beg your pardon?"

"What happens when you take penicillin?"

I thought for a second. "Well, I, uh, kind of broke out in welts and started to stop breathing. I guess if I took it again I would . . . um . . . die?"

The doctor scribbled. "Okay, I'm going to send you home with a scrip for some sulfa. It's a very limited-spectrum antibiotic. Are you still breastfeeding?"

"Yes." Long pause.

"Okay, then." Flip, flip, flip. "How's the Paxil working out?"

"Well, you know." I waited. "I think it's helping, but I still have really bad days maybe two or three times a week."

He put down the chart. "It sounds like an improvement, but that's not really enough for my satisfaction. That might be acceptable for some physicians, but we want you to be better than that."

"Okay," I said. It was hard to argue.

"I'd really like you to consider weaning." He packed up my file and began writing out the scrip. "The prolactin may be influencing your mood."

I'd always heard that prolactin was relaxing. But what did I know? I began taking my sulfa and waiting for my chest to clear up.

I didn't notice much of a change until three nights later, when I couldn't sleep. I felt restless. I was having weird dreams. I kept kicking off the blankets, then huddling up, freezing. I slunk through the next morning, a Sunday, collapsing in a pile while Jim and Baldo went to the grocery store to pick up foodstuffs and items for the Oscar party we had planned with Aunt Erin.

Jim came home from the store. "Do you feel better?" he asked curtly.

"I can't seem to wake up," I whined. I couldn't get out of bed.

Meanwhile, Baldo screamed and clung to me.

That afternoon I went to review *Boat Trip*, a colossal extrusion of a movie starring Oscar winner Cuba Gooding, Jr. as a hapless romantic stuck aboard a gay ocean cruise with his loathsome friend, Horatio Sanz. At one point, Gooding masturbates out the window of his stateroom and inadvertently ejaculates on the face of some poor guy sitting at the bar. I've seen shit movies before, but this one was literally making me sick. The air conditioning was up too high, and I shrank into my seat to conserve my body heat. Some asshole was laughing hysterically at the antics of *Playboy* Playmate Victoria Silvstedt, cast as the linchpin of something called the Swedish Tanning Team. I could feel my gums shrinking. I was thirsty. I put down my pen and tucked my arms inside my sleeves.

I staggered out to the lobby a painful ninety minutes later. The lobby was floating, as if I were looking through waves of heat or gasoline fumes. I had to put both hands on the railing to get up the three stairs to the exit. Outside, the sun was so bright and soothing that I sat in the car with the windows cranked, the visors up, trying to figure out how to get the key in the ignition. Was it upside down? I turned my head to check behind me for traffic, and it was like moving through water with tracers in my field of vision. It was not unpleasant. Warm and fluid, like the womb. I laughed airily as I floated onto the highway.

I rolled up in the driveway and stumbled inside. "Something's weird with me."

The thermometer read 101 degrees. Jim sighed. "It's like you're always *sick*," he said, irritated.

"I don't mean to be."

Exasperated. "I know, but I was really looking forward to this party."

"I'll still watch the awards with you." But I was in bed asleep before the supporting actor was announced.

I spent the next day tucked under a blanket, lying on my side in the living room, trying to read to Baldo and play with him. My feet would poke out and I would mutter. I tried to interest him in a *Baby Einstein* DVD so I could hold still for a while and rest. Not working. Baldo wanted loving ministrations: nursing, reading, holding.

I spent the morning of the next day trying to convince Jim to come home from work and take me to Urgent Care. I couldn't drive myself. I couldn't wrangle Baldo in the waiting room.

The urgent care nurse took my temperature. "One hundred and three degrees," she said, scribbling. The doctor diagnosed me with the flu and sent us all home with instructions to drink Gatorade and finish the sulfa.

That evening, halfway through my third bottle of Gatorade, I noticed a pinprick rash starting on my feet. I took Benadryl and went to bed.

When Baldo woke us the next day, the rash had spread all over. I was almost uniformly pink, as if a tiny pointillist had been stippling on me all night.

"Please stay home," I begged Jim. "Something is wrong with me."

"Something's always wrong with you."

Again, I couldn't argue. "I think I have something worse than the flu. Could I have been bitten by a tick?"

"A tick?"

"Yeah . . . like the ones that carry Rocky Mountain spotted fever?"

Jim relented, and off we went to Urgent Care. Again.

"Hey, you're back!" the phlebotomist greeted me. She tied me off and took another sample.

I was actually feeling better when the phone rang and a different doctor told me my liver levels were 300 percent too high. I needed to check myself into the hospital. I drove myself over to the parking garage and floated over to Admitting.

The intake clerk noted my occupation as "housewife" and sent a septuagenarian volunteer over with a squeaky wheelchair. We squeaked up to the seventh floor.

I'd never been admitted to a hospital as a sick person, only as a laboring one. It was an exciting occasion. I had cable. My phone rang almost constantly, with one well-wisher or another asking if I'd eaten tainted oysters or been bitten by a deer tick. Jim brought a bag with my breast pump and tarot cards in it. I did a reading for my night-shift nurse. I got IV fluids. I tried to watch MTV but found it unbearable. I did manage VH-1.

My friend Michelle came to visit almost immediately, proffering a chocolate bar, trashy books, and a pink flowered blanket. She distracted me with jokes while the nurses dug around in the back of my hand for a vein. She sat in the visitor's chair with an expression of venesectional eagerness. I'm sure I had it, too.

"This is the first time I've been out without kids," she confessed. Ever? Not since her second son was born almost two years ago. "I got to drive over here *all by myself.*"

This was the first time I'd be away from Baldo overnight. No baby. All night long. No night nursing. No early rising. No pooped-in diapers. No cereal to mix. Nothing. Just me and my giant, inflamed liver.

I was so dehydrated that my pumping sessions yielded miserable output: an ounce if I was lucky. I cried, fearful that Baldo would wean. I watched *Trading Spaces.* I had an abdominal ultrasound. It hurt to cough or laugh or talk. I could feel my liver pushing up against my ribs.

The food was almost inedible, but it arrived without any effort on my part. When I was finished, someone took it away. I drank real coffee. There was cake for dessert, and that was all right.

I worried about Jim, at home with Baldo and my mom. Was the baby taking the sippy cup? Was he screaming for me? They came to visit the second day, and Baldo pulled on the electrical cords, rang the nurse's call button accidentally, and tried to climb into the machinery of the adjustable bed. The visits were exhausting. His beady eyes peered up at me from the side of the bed. I'd find myself up and moving around, distracting him, supervising.

Finally they left, and I talked the day nurse into a Benadryl for my itching and slept for sixteen hours straight.

The infectious disease specialist awakened me by flipping my light on and off.

"*Mmmhhp,*" I grunted.

"Rise and shine. I let you sleep the last two times I did my rounds."

"Oh." It was the middle of the next day.

"Let's talk about your health history." He flipped through my chart.

"Okay."

He asked me how much alcohol I drank. I told him I'd have maybe a couple of ounces of wine once or twice a week.

He put down his pen. "Are you telling me the truth?"

"Of course I am," I snapped. "Jesus Christ. I'm a lactating mother. How much am I going to drink?" All these men were starting to piss me off.

"All right, then." He shut my folder. "We're going to keep you hydrated and check your levels one last time. We'll discharge you then, and you can go back to check up with your regular physician."

My regular physician. The one who prescribed the sulfa? The one who thought breastfeeding caused PPD? The one who knew nothing about the past two days—the high fever, the exhaustion? I was going to have to explain all this to him and persuade him to check my liver levels?

"The hell you are." I pointed at the specialist. "I'm not going in to see my doctor. He doesn't know anything about this. I'm staying right here. And I'm not going to see a third doctor at Urgent Care, either. I'm not telling this story to another person."

The doctor went out to the hall to confer with my nurse.

"Okay," he said. "We've decided to keep you in one more night and do the tests in the morning."

"Thank you."

For another twelve hours I slept, hooked up to IV fluids. I can imagine nothing more magical in the life of a new mother than the combination of uninterrupted sleep and intravenous hydration. My medically managed birth experience had soured me on hospitals, but I was willing to reconsider.

I did wake up long enough to express milk, fearful of losing my supply. I'd sit in the recliner, watching the Austin Music Network and pumping. One of the day nurses observed my lactation rig.

"Are you postpartum?" he asked.

"I guess so." It had been over a year now. Still tired, still crazy. Does a woman ever stop being postpartum?

At home Jim had been flooded with offers of help. His fellow teachers were taking off work to come over and have shifts with the baby—holding, feeding, changing. My mother was there.

"I guess we're going to chalk this one up to a really weird drug reaction." The specialist closed my chart for good. I'd long since grown accustomed to hinky little diagnoses: I had really weird ovaries, really weird moods, and now a really weird little liver. Months later, a chiropractor would tell me that liver dysfunction is not uncommon among new mothers; it's associated with something called maternal depletion syndrome. (Talk about putting a name to the obvious.) I still felt like hammered shit.

And so the volunteer rolled me back down to the hospital entrance, where I minded Baldo while Jim paid us out. Baldo kept climbing into the manicured flower beds in the hospital courtyard.

"That is for flowers," I mumbled. The horizon was wobbly. "Let's run around on the sidewalk instead."

The next morning, Jim went back to work, my mother went home, and no one offered to take off work to help me.

HELL

May 6, 2003

The baby is fifteen months old.

I could have done it today, but I didn't.

We were all tired. I'd stayed up late working on an assignment for the paper. They'd sent me to a screening of *A Mighty Wind*, the Christopher Guest folk-music satire. I could have gotten out of it, but I wanted to go. Erin was with me. The crowd was split between boisterous aging hippies and twentysomething emo couples with matching horn-rims. It was nice. But when I came home, I spent too much time writing and wasn't asleep until after midnight.

Jim woke me a little before five and handed me our squirming, whimpering toddler. "He's been up and down all night," he mumbled.

Baldo held on to me and cried all morning. He held me and cried through one failed morning nap, then another. We nursed and rocked, nursed and rocked. Hours passed. I had to put him in his crib and let him cry so I could email my completed work to my editor before noon.

My baby sitter, Briony, and her son came by. She took a step back when she saw me.

"I'd really like to get out today." I said. It was a wish, not a statement.

We tried for another nap. No dice. More crying and fussing and clutching of legs. Briony held out her arms. "Just go," she said. I handed off my screaming and crying baby and collected my keys. What could I do?

Out I went, into the rain on the highway, the slick Highway 183 flyover, with its high concrete guardrails and shitty drivers. There was little traffic; I could pick a lane and take care of everything.

Instead I went north into the suburbs and took an exit off the elevated. I pulled over into the parking lot of the public library. It was nicely appointed, with plentiful, well-marked parking spaces and a tasteful brown brick exterior. (My own neighborhood branch was in a dingy storefront next to an interior fabrics store; a cadaver had recently been discovered in the Dumpster.) Maybe there'd be plush chairs, the white noise of humming hard drives and whistling air-conditioning. No people with bedrolls and liquid coughs. Quiet stacks where I could lose myself amidst the selections of a far-flung branch: 1980s cookbooks, outdated computing manuals, uplifting celebrity memoirs.

Something was wrong. The plentiful parking spaces were full of minivans. One of them sported a decal across the rear window: HONEY BEE QUILTING. Quilting? Minivans? I was instantly furious. I hated these people just by looking at their cars. Quilting. Aren't there enough quilts already? Why are people still making more? How many quilts does the world need? Fuck quilts.

Inside you couldn't swing a cadaver without hitting a Peter Rabbit diaper bag or a Tupperware full of Cheerios. Toddlers with matching socks were jabbering and walking independently. Their mothers were prepared. They had umbrellas, operational ones. (Mine, a crumpled hand-me-down printed with a map of the London Underground, was under the driver's seat with Baldo's winter hat and half the soil from my tomato plants.) These were Those Other Mothers. Their children were laughing and having enriching social experiences. Mine was at home, squalling in the arms of a baby sitter. I ran away from my child. I was a piece of shit.

I couldn't think of what else to do, so I checked out a copy of *You'll Never Make Love in This Town Again*, the Hollywood hooker tell-all, and Richard Ferber's *Solving Your Child's Sleep Problems*. Why not? And then I did the only constructive thing I could imagine: I sat down to write, using a ballpoint from the bottom of my purse (it was a "gimme" pen from the condo we stayed in during our honeymoon on Maui—how long had it been there?) and five of those little scraps of paper they put in boxes by the computers so you can jot down call numbers. Fortunately, they were double sided.

> *I am chickenshit for not going ahead with it. I am brave for fighting it.*
>
> *I am a shitty mother for wanting to leave. I am a loving mother for staying.*
>
> *I am damaging my child with my sickness. I am teaching my child with my survival.*

I left after I'd filled all five pages. The sun had come out, and the highway was drying. I came through the door to the sound of my child laughing. I closed it, and he began sobbing hysterically.

"He's been fine. He just started," Briony said. They know, she said, that we are their comfort. They feel safe enough to fall apart around us. They hide their frustrations from everyone but show them to us.

I tried to feed Baldo lunch. I put him in his high chair while he was still crying and gave him some toast and fruit and began making a sandwich. Over and over, I told him what I was doing, that I was hungry, that I needed to eat, too.

I'm sorry, I'm sorry, I'm sorry, I said.

AND ON THAT FARM
THERE WAS A CRAZY
POSTPARTUM WOMAN

I'M SITTING AT MY PARENTS' ELDERLY Compaq Presario 7222, which has Novell PerfectWorks installed. It's midmorning on a Sunday, so my mother is folding her whites. After a half-hour of fussing, my son has fallen asleep and remained so during two rings of the doorbell: a townie wanting to buy round bales of the Bermuda coastal hay my parents grow on their farm outside of Bellville, Texas, population 3,500.

Last Friday
Allow me to explain how I came to be here.

It was a day like any other, with crying and fussing and screaming—Baldo's and mine. With Jim at school, we were alone together, and I'd reached my limit.

I bundled the baby into the car and went for a drive. Nowhere in particular, just anywhere. I realized I was heading down Lamar Boulevard to Erin's house. I cried at every red light. I cried whenever I got stopped behind a bus. I cried when a bicyclist entered my lane. I cried when I hit construction, and I cried when I hit the school zone in Erin's neighborhood. The crossing guard stopped me and made full-on eye contact, and I wondered if it was unusual for crazy women in station wagons to be sobbing uncontrollably at her intersection. Probably not.

And here were these young children teeming everywhere, wearing brilliant, clean cotton juvenile separates and earthy sandals and swinging lunchboxes and leaping into the arms of their well-educated urbanite parents, these BoBos with graying hair and respectable vocations and string bags full of organic produce from the locally owned market down the street. I was furious, positively furious at these people, these fucking stupid people with their wonderful children who weren't crying, and their lives were so happy and rewarding and full of love, and I wanted to yank my baby out of his car seat and leave him on the curb because I wasn't a mother. I fucking hate Erin's neighborhood. Erin wasn't even there, or at least she wasn't answering the door. I rolled down the windows and sat at her curb, crying for twenty minutes and wondering how I was going to make it back home, across town.

I know what I would have done if she had been at home and I could have left him there. I would have done it.

Instead I took the freeway and literally floored it, which I'd never done in a car before, and got up to eighty on the onramp and thought about every bridge and elevated, every guardrail I could break, every hospital or fire station I could stop at, every place I could leave the baby without fear of prosecution. Or maybe I could keep driving north, go to Dallas, get a job at an ad agency or an airline magazine and send money home to Baldo and Jim to pay for a nanny. Live in a cheapjack apartment by myself and watch cable.

I wanted to ask someone which was the worst: living with a crazy mother, being a child of divorce, or having a dead parent. Those were my three options. I'm already hurting him; I'm already abusing him every time I lose my grip and yell at him to shut up, every time I run a red light on purpose, every time I sit on the floor and stare into the fireplace while he throws books at me and bellows. Every time he sits in his crib crying for an hour instead of falling asleep, which he'd done twice that day; I abuse him.

Later that day, I called the county crisis line and talked to a male counselor while Baldo was pulling Kleenex out of the box and ripping them into diaphanous shreds.

"What can I do for you?" he asked.

"I don't know," I said. "What do you do?"

"We can talk about your problem and solutions to it," he said.

Poor guy. Probably an intern from UT. Probably some twenty-three-year-old guy who'd never even had a conversation with a postpartum woman. He called me by my name a lot, as if negotiating with terrorists. Every statement started with, "I hear that . . . "

"You say that you want to kill yourself, Marrit, but I hear that you're trying to find a way to get better. That's why you've been to the doctor; that's why you're calling me now, Marrit," he said.

What is it with these people that they think they can outsmart you? Catch you in an act of double-think, get you to admit you're not actually suicidal, and that'll be the end of it?

"Of course I want to get better," I said. "Nothing is helping. Not therapy. Not medication. What else is there? What else can I do besides kill myself or run away?"

"Have you had a break from the baby?" he finally asked.

"Well, I was in the hospital for two days with hepatitis," I said.

There is another hospital, it turns out, for people who are mentally ill and have to be admitted. He told me about it, gave me the address, and essentially hung up. It was the end of the script.

I sat there in my pile of shredded Kleenex. The phone rang again. My dad was on his way. "Don't go anywhere," my mother said. "Don't get in the car. Don't do anything. Just wait for him."

I am so tired.

Monday

I've been on the farm for two nights now. I think I'm getting better. Three pairs of eyes watch intently while I take my Paxil each morning with my coffee. My mother, who has osteoporosis, further insists upon a calcium pill and a vitamin D supplement. My father, wearing his work shirt and gimme cap, lectures me on the importance of finding an analyst once I'm back in Austin. Then he goes out to the hayfield to move his irrigation gun.

Life is different here. Amidst the dually trucks and Suburbans, I feel conspicuous in our Volvo wagon with its pro-choice sticker (though my mother informs me that there is another Volvo in town, a white one—she sees it parked at the grocery store sometimes); I feel like a walking eighteen-gauge nostril piercing as we stop to pick up "buddy" poppies from an elderly VFW volunteer seeking donations for veterans' services. But we fit somehow. Yesterday Mom took me to her stylist, who works out of a storefront salon off of Highway 159 on the way to Sealy, and the two of them convinced me to forego the trim I was considering and get a spiky, butch micro-cut. ("I love your hair," Mom told me this morning. "You look like a mischievous little boy.") I feel chagrined for having underestimated this place.

Last night Jim and I went out on a date. We put Baldo down to sleep after supper and cleaned ourselves up a little. I put wax in my butch hair and borrowed a clean blouse from my mother. Jim changed his drooled-on t-shirt for an aloha. We took a farm road into town and had drinks at the Alibi, a darkened sports lounge next to the Snowflake Bakery on the south side of the historical town square. The barkeep, pregnant and smoking, fixed me a whiskey sour. Jim, denied a beer on tap, had to settle for longnecks. We must have looked like candy-pants out-of-towners shopping for antique bric-a-brac over Memorial Day weekend. We played AC/DC and Stevie Ray Vaughan on the jukebox, and when I was tipsy, Jim persuaded me to shoot pool, which I'd never done before. I kept forgetting whether I was stripes or solids, and I scratched a lot, but I think I acquitted myself estimably for a neophyte. One across-the-table shot elicited the bartender's approval; another got me a nod from the bar's two other patrons, who were talking with a guy selling homemade jerky out of his car for $5 a bag.

We stopped off at a gas station on the way home, and Jim got some beer for us to take home and drink under the stars, where we'd be less likely to be killed by other motorists. I waited in the car and watched the locals, two by two and three by three, stream in and out. One woman fueled up on her way home from work, still wearing her camp shirt from a fast food restaurant, but the rest were all men buying beers and cigarettes and dipping tobacco. According to Jim, the following conversation transpired:

CLERK: So what's going on tonight?

GUY: I'm tired. I've been workin' my ass off all day.

CLERK: So you goin' on home?

GUY: Naw, I'm goin' out.

CLERK: To Houston (some hour and a half away on the interstate)?

GUY: Nope, I'm goin' to Hempstead (some forty-five minutes away on the state highway).

CLERK: What's goin' on in Hempstead?

GUY: I dunno. Gonna find out.

We thought it peculiar (and somewhat alarming) that someone would drive to another town, after a full day of work, with no particular plans and a six-pack of beer in progress, but we are candy-pants out-of-towners who live within walking distance of a *raspas* stand, a karaoke bar, a dim sum restaurant, a yoga studio, a public library, a gut-busting barbecue place, a purveyor of exotic fish, a head shop, a thrift store, a home-brew supplier, and a city bus line. We do not understand these things. So we went back home hastily and sat in the back of my father's pickup playing "Geek," a round-robin game that tests the players' knowledge of film stars and directors. Our intermittent attempts at romantic engagement were thwarted by my father, who'd pop out from time to time to sneak a cigarette or call the cat. It was like being sixteen again.

*

Tuesday

By the time Monday morning's nap went kaput, we were sick of rusticity and desperate for shoppertainment. We loaded our wired, over-tired toddler into the car, attempting to induce a nap, and drove the hour and a half east to Houston, home of the nearest IKEA.

A nice lesbian couple applauded my parenting as I changed the baby's diaper on the floor of the tiny bathroom, laying him across my lower body instead of the floor. The much-heralded "baby room" was locked, even after I flagged an employee who disappeared into the bowels of the Employees Only area in search of a key and stayed gone for twenty minutes. Slumped on a bench, I watched older children admitted to the "ball room," which also offered easels and piles of books and uniformed childcare workers. A grateful father made eye contact with me after his sweet, pageboyed six-year-old daughter skipped off into the room, as if to say "You'll get there." But we weren't yet. We were in a giant retail Shangri-La, where the snacks were forbidden (certainly there were eggs in the *kothbullar*) and the height requirement was too high and the elevator was full and the walkways were just wide enough to accommodate a tantruming toddler who refused to walk.

I tried to amuse Baldo by placing him atop a furry inflatable ottoman, which collapsed when he rolled over. We took him to the toy department, and he climbed to the back of a wire shelf full of stuffed kittens and refused to come out. Our predecessors in the checkout line took each item out of their cart and paid for it individually, arguing amongst themselves about which roommate would buy which pillow and shelf. Baldo kept flinging his cup to the floor and screaming. A jocular young couple without children laughed toothsomely when I told the baby it was *all gone*. They looked so fucking carefree and adorable that I wanted to pound the shit out of them. Jim and I argued all the way home, while I sat in the back seat and fed Baldo some revolting Gerber meat sticks (I had to drain the jar of its briny fluid in the parking lot) and pieces of unwashed pear, bitten off by me since I, ever unprepared, had no utensils. I am a shit mother.

Tuesday morning's nap was skipped in lieu of an hour of panicked crying. We did everything normally—bath time, massage, sleepytime nursing in the quiet chair—and the first fifteen minutes seemed promising. Quiet babbling, then silence. Then screaming. Screaming. Screaming. Teething tablets. Orajel. Screaming. Screaming. Coughing. Gagging.

I sat on the couch with my parents. We looked at each other as the hour elapsed. I was full of despair.

"You're not the first person this has happened to," my dad pronounced. "I've been through this."

My mom and I looked at each other. I don't think so.

Wednesday

I resolved to get out of the house by myself. Baldo was exhausted by naptime, rubbing his eyes and twisting up furiously. Yet again he refused sleep.

"Just keep him alive," I called over my shoulder as I shut the door. I drove into town.

It's funny to see urban culture permeating small towns. It's funny to see a tiny car-stereo store on a historic town square, its rent-a-sign advising me to "roll phat this summer" with some electronic distraction. I poked around in the town's only bookstore, a locally owned place where the bibliophiles congregate. My mother, a regular, is notorious for having special-ordered the entire Elmore Leonard catalog, piece by piece. I rooted around in the used-books section, wondering who traded in the selections—the Chuck Palahniuk, the William Gibson. Did they belong to a soybean farmer? A high school kid? The town acupuncturist? An equine veterinarian? What kind of asshole was I, wondering if country people read?

I left with two novels and a board book, *The Carrot Seed*, a classic from 1945 about a little boy who plants and tends the titular plant, heedless to the protestations of his naysaying mother, father, and brother. It made me choke up. *My son is a carrot seed!* I wailed inwardly. *I just need to believe in him!* It sounds horribly platitudinous, but I felt better. I looked at the pictures as I sat in the car—the mother in her crinolined housedress, her hair set in waves, her smile so gentle and sympathetic. Inevitably I compared myself: Would I be hanging out the back door in cutoffs, with a Parliament stuck in my mouth and a bottle of Pearl Light? *Forget it, kid—that fucking seed's not gonna grow! Now get your butt back in here and watch* Arthur!

When I'm close to home, I'm in the habit of listening to the cock-rock radio station of my youth because it's so immutable, so firmly entrenched in 1987 that the vagaries of pop music don't make a dent. You'll still be hearing Yngwie Malmsteen and spots for

Rick's Cabaret. The on-air personalities still have names like "The Boner." There's really no reason to listen, aside from the curiosity factor. So I dug around in the CDs and pulled out New Order. And then something started to happen to me.

I'm not a bad mother. I'm not an asshole. Not really, I mean. I'm not perfect, but I love my son. Half the time I don't know what the fuck he's trying to tell me—if his teeth hurt or he's shat his pants, if he's feeling anxious or insecure or gassy or itchy. I didn't magically know I was pregnant at the moment of conception; I thought he was a girl. I'm not intuitive. I can't quiet his tears. We weren't perfectly bonded in dyadic bliss from the moment of his birth. We were in separate rooms as soon as the cord was cut, and yes, that's still totally an issue for me because of this yammering, stupid voice I have in my head that says a mother is everything to her child, at the expense of herself, or else she's a failure, unloving, a piece-of-shit human being. Then she's drowning in her own anger, choking on her bile. Every word she says is an insult, every touch an assault, every silence an affront. She reads the wrong books too often and not enough, and she turns the pages too slowly and too quickly, and she's too lenient and too hard, too distant and too overbearing. She holds him too much and not enough, loves him too much and not enough, hates him and hates herself.

But here was New Order and a blue sky and a clean two-lane road back to my parents' house, and everything seemed better. New Order are survivors. All parents. So Ian Curtis hanged himself because he was depressed and epileptic, but the group cohered and kept going and gained momentum somehow. Even bad New

Order—and here I'm thinking of that song they recorded for the World Cup—is the music of tough bastards. And here was me, listening to that music, hurting and crying for a year and a half, wanting to leave my family or hurt myself because there was no other way to go on. But if I couldn't do these things, I'd just have to fight harder. And then I'd have to forgive myself. I'd have to accept that I was always going to fall short. I was always going to fuck up. I was always going to lose stuff and spill things and leave the house without enough diapers; I was always going to second-guess my decisions. And somehow we were going to get on with it. Baldo wasn't going to grow up to resent me for eating too much pie or not having Waldorf toys or overdosing him with Zantac. And if he did, I'd have to blow it off, because that's asinine. I was just going to have to stick around and do my best. Which is, of course, plenty.

Thursday

I had planned to meet a friend from online, but my mother balked. "Someone you met on the Internet?" she asked incredulously. "Is that safe?" I don't want to tell her that I met all my mother friends online. Women don't just walk up to each other anymore. Moreover, our schedules conflicted, and I was too tired to put up a fight or go anywhere. So my mother and I set my dad up with Baldo, who was fussing and screaming as usual, and went to the area's premier retail outlet and the locus of shoppertainment, Wal-Mart.

I hate Wal-Mart. It is a way of life, however, for rural dwellers, who are compelled to collect caulk and nine-volt batteries and extra shoelaces and tampons and toothpaste and a quart of milk just as we all are, and who are similarly pressed for time and convenience. I understand this, and I'm trying not to be a snob. It's really easy for me to tell them to drive back and forth across the county visiting independent purveyors of hardware, groceries, media, and electronics. But I bitched and groused from the parking lot, where we parked in view of a Chevy Suburban painted to look like a giant American flag unfurling in the wind and emblazoned with the words CAN'T TOUCH THIS, to the pharmacy, where naughty items like condoms and disposable enemas were discreetly stored, and from whence I obtained a three-day supply of generic miconazole suppositories to vanquish the yeast infection exacerbating my dyspepsia. (My mom collared a stammering elderly male clerk to inquire, "Where is the Monistat?" but he could only point us toward a cream for anal pruritus.) I ranted about artificial colors and flavors and bovine hormones in the dairy aisle, where the organic full-fat baby yogurt had been replaced with a Disney brand that was green and blue. But I managed to keep my mouth shut while we picked out a footed-pajamas pattern and seven yards of cotton fabric; Mom had offered to sew lightweight summer full-coverage sleepwear so Baldo couldn't scratch his eczema in the night. Not only am I a shitty mother, but I can't even thread the needle in my sewing machine.

We returned to find my father asleep on the couch and Baldo sacked out in his crib. The baby had fallen asleep on the floor. Now I owe my father $1,000.

Friday
On Friday we drove home, surrounded on all sides by people en

route to the Republic of Texas biker rally. Baldo laughed and laughed at the noisy motors.

The next morning he began walking on his own, pumping his arms above his head like a West Coast rapper.

BIRTH EXPERIENCE **BINGO**

"SAY NO TO A CAESAREAN!" screamed the banner headline of *Mothering* magazine, "the magazine of natural family living." *Adbusters*, which purports to "challenge the commercial forces eroding our physical, cultural, and mental environments and offer a radical rethink of our society's unsustainable course," warned readers in a pithy featurette that mammals whose offspring were surgically delivered "reject their babies" because they lack sufficient mothering hormones; thus, we too should not undergo caesareans. The *Flagstaff Tea Party*, "a community forum for the discussion of progressive ideas," featured a first-person account by Jill Ainsworth, entitled "Hypnotherapist Works Overtime to Help Mother Avoid Caesarean."

Meanwhile, the caesarean section surges in popularity. At the time of this writing, the overall rate of caesarean delivery in the United States hovers at 26 percent, an all-time high, and higher than the safety standards recommended by the World Health Organization. More than 600,000 women are having caesareans every year. And in October of 2003, the American College of Obstetricians and Gynecologists (ACOG) published an opinion (entitled "Surgery and Patient Choice: The Ethics of Decision Making") supporting practitioners who perform caesareans despite a lack of "medical necessity"—in other words, elective caesareans. The statement ignited a blaze of controversy, with vaginal-birth advocates chiding ACOG for a "carte blanche" approach to surgical birthing.

In the popular media much was made of the rise in these so-called "patient-choice" caesareans—ones requested by the birthing mothers, rather than recommended by providers. Celebrities (such as Elizabeth Hurley and Victoria Beckham) and "professional women" were said to prefer the surgical option because it was less messy and icky and was perceived to reduce the damage to their girly parts. *TIME* quoted the British tabloids' trumpeting of "Too Posh to Push."[16] Indeed, a frequently cited study from HealthGrades in July 2003 pointed out that the rate of patient-choice caesarean in the United States had risen 20 percent between 1999 and 2001. Visions of snooty fashionista mothers dropping in by the thousands to deliver after afternoon tea filled the minds of an angry public. Yet patient-choice caesarean still comprised only 1.87 percent of all deliveries in 2001 at the end of the study. Melinda Tuhus, writing in *Women's eNews*, suggests another reason for the high rate of caesarean: "In an effort to avoid being sued, obstetricians are increasingly delivering babies by caesarean section, if fetal monitoring shows the slightest abnormality."

The vast majority of women delivering by caesarean, in other words, do so not by choice, but by necessity (or at least perceived necessity on the part of their healthcare providers). These women are the same ones who will encounter *Mothering* and *Adbusters* at the co-op. They will most likely have one of two reactions: stubborn disdain for the procedure (which has legitimate advantages in some instances and should exist as an option) or shame. Which one of these is more counterproductive?

In the first case, your primary objective as a birthing mother will be "avoiding the caesarean," not delivering a healthy baby. If you relent and accept a "section" from your scalpel-loving, lawsuit-fearing obstetrician, you are, from the start, an "inferior" mother—you chose the option more convenient for your provider and more harmful to your child, and you lack those "mothering hormones" afterward.

Yet again, mothers just can't win. Your doctor wants you to have a caesarean more than ever, we're told. But you must say no.

Dig around in the collections of "birth stories" posted on the Internet, and again and again you will hear "success stories" and tales of "good births." In other words, these people *said NO to a caesarean.* "I felt the satisfaction of birthing my babies," says one woman who was being prepped for surgery but managed to squeeze out her twins under the wire. "I start crying tears of joy," another beams during her present-tense story of a stalled labor. "Finally my body is doing something (albeit drug-induced), and I am not going to have to have a C-section!"

If you read stories of caesarean births, you may notice an apologetic or defensive tone. "I didn't want to have a C-section, of course," writes one mother, "but considering how things were going, it was the most prudent route, especially with the meconium. I still regret not seeing him at the moment of his birth and not being able to hold him much or nurse him [until] the next day." Another writes, "The feeling of failing because of the C-section still (almost seven years later) has not completely gone." Most women contrast a caesarean with "natural birth"—not "vaginal birth"—even when they agree that the surgery was medically necessary in their case and otherwise express no regrets.

So here are all these mothers—some of them with ruptured placentas, some of them with preeclampsia, some of them with toxemia—still referring to their babies' "births" in quotation marks. Still lugging around the baggage of their surgery. Still trying to heal.

I would not deny any woman her own authentic feelings after a surgical birth—I was furious after mine—but I rankle when anyone divides mothers into those who "have birthed" and those who have "been sectioned." Here again we see Procrustean binary logic applied to the experience of mothering: We either "progress" or we "fail"; our bodies are either "competent" or "incompetent"; our births are either "natural" or "medicated" or "surgical." The language used to describe us by both allopathic medicine and natural-birth advocates—language we ourselves adopt and employ—misrepresents the vast possibilities of birthing. A mother who labors without analgesics and delivers in a tub or on a stool is heroic, giving her baby a "gentle birth" and the "best start." A mother who is induced, receives Stadol or an epidural, or delivers in an operating room is "weak," "poorly informed," or "unable to advocate" for the best interests of her child.

When I was forty-one weeks pregnant and my OB was starting to make noise about induction, I sat down at my computer and typed out a journal entry releasing all my feelings about the possibilities of the birth. What exactly was I afraid of? I wasn't afraid of pain, of stronger Pitocin-related contractions. I wasn't afraid of complications. I wasn't afraid of a longer recovery. My feelings, I discovered, had little to do with the baby at all, though I did worry that we wouldn't "bond" and breastfeed immediately as good mothers did. I worried that a physician would push me around. I worried that I would be unable to meet the expectations I had placed on myself. I worried about my own weaknesses. I worried about being judged. I worried about deviating from my birth plan. I worried about beginning my journey into motherhood on a sour note. Postsurgical pain didn't even occur to me. I feared the caesarean as proof of my own inability to parent. I "knew" that if I "capitulated" and agreed to be induced, I would inevitably slide down a slippery slope into further interventions—an epidural that would slow my labor, "failure to progress," and a caesarean. Statistically speaking, there are reasons behind this fear. Philosophically, I objected to the medicalization of the birth process for healthy childbearing women. And I still do. But when I sat down to write my feelings, I released a stream of bile that was horribly, surprisingly antiwoman.

Women who have caesareans are stupid, I wrote. *They are poorly educated.* Of course I was wrong to equate "stupid" with "poorly educated," but did I really believe any of it? Apparently I did. *They let male or male-identified doctors push them into a preferred outcome.* Thus I discovered that I wasn't really angry at the medical establishment at all. I willingly transferred my anger to its "victims"—individual women, the kind I purported to support as a feminist, even if their lives and choices and outcomes were unlike mine. I eagerly separated myself from women who accepted interventions and birthed surgically. I wasn't "like them." I was smart and prepared and self-aware. That wouldn't happen to me. I was immune from the dangers because I read the right books, knew the right people, held the right beliefs. And so I demonized the people affected by the system I disdained, just as a juror might blame a rape survivor for her assault. (That I would automatically compare a surgical birth to an assault was itself telling.)

I wanted to rise from my child-bed like a birthing goddess. I wanted my friends and family to applaud me and admire my strength. I didn't want my home-birthing acquaintances to cluck their tongues at me, to feel sorry for me, to pity a baby born to a woman who was less than strong. "Wasn't it wonderful?" they'd ask. "Oh, it was hard," I'd say. "But I stuck by my beliefs."

Where in all of this was the baby?

If doctors interfered with my birth, surely I would wind up flat on my back in a hospital bed, benumbed and unable to nurse my child. And of course he'd get nipple confusion instantly; he'd scream in a plastic bassinet and be tended to by strangers. I'd have to buy formula and feed him from Playtex nursers. Women would glare at me in public. Breastfeeding advocates would plaster FORMULA IS POISON! stickers on the shelves at the grocery store and remind me that my baby would perform more poorly on standardized tests and suffer allergies later in life.

I would be like those other "stupid" women—one of whom was my own mother, who birthed in twilight sleep and fed both her babies formula without a second thought.

Fortunately, nature has a way of disabusing us of our misapprehensions. And so when my water broke, when I was nine centimeters dilated after a perfect Hollywood-movie labor during which I practiced yoga and sat upright, the nurse reached in and felt my son's butt.

"The baby's breech," she said. "And I can't remember the last time I saw so much mec."

The attending doctor was not my own. She was better. She was surrounded by a violet glow. I looked at her with pleading eyes and saw a women's volleyball coach, cheering me on to a championship victory. Slightly butch. Infinitely trustworthy. And I had let her down.

"Man!" she yelled, smacking her palms on the cart. "I am so bummed!"

"Me too," I said.

I turned to Jim, who was lost at sea somewhere and had been since I awoke with strong, regular contractions at four thirty that morning. He was off in the clouds while we parked in the hospital garage and I insisted—demanded—that he leave the engine on long enough for me to hear the end of "Singular Girl" by Old 97's, which was playing on the radio. I had to hear it. It meant everything. He looked at me blankly as I curled up on my right side and gripped the gurney in our labor and delivery suite and barked out orders for gum.

"Are you sure you want to be in that position? That's not from class, is it?"

"Get me gum!" I had to be chewing gum in that position. "I'm doing yoga!"

When we all realized the baby was breech, Jim's face was expressionless again. And everyone was looking at me.

I experienced a clarity of vision unlike almost any other in my lifetime, even though the contractions felt as if a giant invisible hand were crumpling me up and throwing me against the wall. My mind was as lucid as it had been in the eighth grade when I won the UIL Readywriting competition with a crystalline essay on violence in the media, trouncing my too-competitive best friend.

"Okay, people," I said. They huddled around me, my teammates. "What's safest for the baby at this point?"

The doctor and the nurse exchanged looks. "I don't know about a vaginal breech birth for a first-time mom," the doctor said. Technically an endorsement of the surgery, but far from the pushiest statement I'd ever heard from a physician.

Did I argue? Nope. "All right then," I said. "Let's go to the OR." And then I hit transition.

I screamed unselfconsciously all the way down the hall. The head of a kindly anesthesiologist popped up into view.

"Hi," it said. "My name's Brendan."

"Hi, Brendan," I said. "How's it going?" And I screamed. My birth was officially fucked up, so there was no point in keeping up appearances.

Somebody rolled me onto my side. A spinal block went in one hole, a morphine drip in another. I should point out that I have not been a stranger to such substances, so I wasn't surprised when I started to itch.

"Damn, I'm itchy. And what's this shoulder thing?"

"You may feel some pressure there," Brendan said.

"That feels funny," I said. "I love you."

Suddenly Jim stood beside me in a showercap. I laughed. "Dude, you're wearing a showercap." Then the contours of his face started to change. His cheeks became hollow. Pockmarks appeared, studded with little white buds. He was turning into a potato.

"God, I'm tripping," I moaned. Why now? "I'm sorry, but I can't look at you. Okay? It's freaking me out."

Somebody was tugging at me. I turned this way and that underneath the drape.

"Do you want that drape there?" Jim asked. No doubt, he recalled from birthing class that I could watch the procedure if I wanted to.

"Fuck, yes."

I turned his way.

"Oh, cool!" Jim blurted.

"Here's the butt!" the doctor said.

Somebody was crying. It was Baldo.

"It's a boy."

"It is?" I'd been expecting a little girl named Audrey.

They were aspirating him, weighing him, whisking him from the room. At that point, I guess I should have become indignant. I should have demanded to see him. I should have demanded to bond with him. But I was still hallucinating. What if the baby turned into a snail or something? *That* would be a bad start.

More tugging followed. I lay there, bored. So that was it. I'd failed. Well, close the book on this one. Nurse Ratchet was probably stuffing a Nuk into the kid's mouth or giving him a Happy Meal. Hooking him up to an IV of Kool-Aid. He'd have to grow up in an iron lung. Maybe the other kids would use him as third base. He'd call me "Mother," and I'd sign his college tuition checks while he snuggled with a rhesus monkey made of sheepskin. He'd write a tell-all memoir: "She was tripping when I was born!"

Then there he was. Two pink cheeks underneath a striped cap in his father's arms.

"Oh, cool," I whispered. "Look at that. It's a baby."

Then he screamed.

I'd like to tell you that the instant I looked into his eyes, I laid aside all of my attitudes about caesarean birth and became a better person. But that didn't happen. Instead, I spent three hours in recovery, unable to feel my legs. I felt angry with my body for refusing to wake up. I couldn't feed it until it farted. It ached like never before—I'd never had surgery before. I couldn't stand up. I couldn't lie down on my side. I couldn't change Baldo's diaper. Someone would have to put him in my arms, and I'd sit there stiffly in the adjustable bed, feeling about as maternal as a starfish. Already I'd fucked everything up. I wept rivers. I was stapled shut. I had to cough into a pillow. Jim stayed beside me day and night, sleeping lightly in the room's horrible cushioned window seat.

Each day a different doctor came to inspect my incision—all women, all mothers. They all acted like it was no big deal. I wanted to beg them to disapprove of me. But they scribbled in my folder and vanished. On the last day, I got my discharge from a spunky OB with permed hair and running shoes. She noted our bag of organic snacks from Whole Foods Market, the weekly newspaper on the floor.

"Cool," she said, scribbling.

Was she approving of me? But I'd failed! I brought Recharge instead of Gatorade, and I still fucked up.

She checked my incision. "That looks awesome. Michelle did a great job."

Awesome? It was horrific and disfiguring.

"You did a great job, too."

I went home to heal. When I stepped through the door, my mother met me with a pair of scissors. She cut the hospital bracelet off my arm and held me.

When we'd finally fallen into a pattern of napping and nursing— a pattern that would soon be disrupted by the onset of reflux—I went promptly to an online community for mothers, prepared to give my confession as a failed birther and beg for absolution. I was accustomed to the posters whose signatures proclaimed their two home births, their refusal to circumcise, their belief in natural medicine. I would throw myself upon my sword before them. They would pity me and my child, and my suffering would begin in earnest.

"I said yes to a caesarean," I wrote. And I sat back to watch the disapproval begin.

It never did.

Instead, I heard stories like mine. Some of them were bitter, make no mistake. And it's reasonable, I think, to be angry if a bunch of people barked orders at you while you were laboring in great pain, pronounced you a failure, and subjected you to major abdominal surgery, if that is indeed what happened to you. But I also heard a lot of relief. *I'm so glad I can finally talk about this,* women wrote. *I was so afraid of being judged.* So many people piled on to tell their caesarean stories that we threatened to crash the site's database.

We were all afraid of being judged. There's that word again. Judgment is a leitmotif of motherhood—along with guilt. Neither feeling is constructive; neither comforts your child or fills you with energy or feeds people. You will feel judged regardless of your particular choices. If you are having a hospital birth with a physician, you will be judged as retrograde and out of touch with your body. If you are having a home birth with a midwife, you will be judged as insane and a threat to your baby. I watched a mother of two—a student midwife—collapse into tears of gratitude when she was finally able to confess that she had her son circumcised because penile cancer runs in her family; in fact, she'd recently watched her father die from it. I've seen women who refused circumcision branded as controlling bitches putting their children at risk for the sake of their politics. Get the eye ointment and be judged; refuse it and be judged. Vaccinate and be judged; don't vaccinate and be judged (as well as kicked out of your pediatric practice and your preschool).

And this is what makes us crazy. Not caesarean birth, *per se,* but the feeling that we have failed in spite of ourselves, a feeling that will inevitably strike all of us. The feeling that our choices were taken from us and made by other people, a feeling that hardly begins and ends with the medical establishment but is engendered whenever people push mothers around. We are the straw women others batter high-mindedly: We are "too posh"— isn't it horrible? We are "too stubborn"—isn't that awful? We are "too passive"—don't we know anything? Don't we know how to say no? We are depressed because we are poised on the brink of doom. Because everyone around us is anticipating disaster, our feelings of powerlessness—failure, incompetence—blossom into self-loathing and rage.

They strip us of our power. And we help them do it.

FUCK DR. SEARS, OR THE FALLACY OF DESIGNER PARENTING

"I'M KNOCKED UP," I intoned into the phone to my mother, waving my pee stick with the two pink lines.

"Now everyone will be telling you what to do. Including me," she said. "Don't listen." With that, she handed the phone to my father.

Of course she was right. Everyone had opinions about my gestation and our plans for raising a sprout.

"Do what you want, just don't homeschool," said my father, who was pretty opinionated about maternity for a hay farmer. "And nurse for six months. That's plenty."

"What is the baby? A girl, right?" asked a coworker when I was perhaps eight weeks pregnant, as if we could tell. As if the embryo was sexually differentiated.

"What's your theme? You gotta have a theme," declared one of Jim's colleagues, an oft-repeated question we finally began answering sarcastically: *We're going with an authentic biker-bar motif. We're seasoning the walls with Vantage 100s to give them a rich tobacco patina, and we're going to scatter muddy sawdust around the concrete floor. The baby will sleep on a splintery picnic table or pass out in the corner.*

"That's going to be twins!" announced a guy at the grocery

store, pointing at what was by then my third-trimester belly, while he was stocking lemons. He could not be disabused of this notion, despite our multiple ultrasounds.

"You're gonna need the epidural," said the checker at Home Depot who was ringing up my new faucet.

All men. All opinionated. None of them the primary caregiver for a child. Sound familiar?

We got our first book from the "experts" on loan from some friends. It was William Sears's *The Baby Book*. I liked it. It seemed to validate what I suspected, despite my increasing anxiety and paranoia: I was properly invested with all the emotional and physical tools necessary to raise a happy, healthy child. I should trust my instincts and do what felt natural. Tasteful, pleasant line drawings depicted a smiling mother with a neat bob nursing, fastening her sling, playing with cylindrical foam bolster pillows, and otherwise assisting her babbling, secure infant on its journey through life. How reassuring! We would be attachment parents. We spouted Sears-isms in birthing class, scanning the faces of the other couples for signs of recognition. We brought our copy with us to the hospital, where the lactation consultant swooned over it. All was good. Except for one thing.

"That Dr. Sears is a kook," my mother proclaimed.

"No, you're thinking of Barry Sears, the diet guy," I corrected.

"I know who I mean."

Having been given dispensation to ignore her, I chose to. Soon the baby began vomiting great torrents of half-digested breast milk.

"Uh oh, it's not supposed to be projectile," I told Jim.

"Why is that bad?"

"I don't know, but look at this list—that's bad."

The baby began screaming and twisting up like a fortune-telling fish after every feeding.

"No, he's supposed to drift off peacefully at the breast." I pointed to the picture.

"That's not peaceful."

"I know."

We tried the colic maneuvers. We bicycled legs. We swung the baby around on our forearms. Nothing seemed to help. Worse, it was happening all day.

Finally I devised a baby-joggling maneuver based on Dr. Sears's advice to move the baby in more than one plane (say, bounce up and down and forward and backward at the same time). I would joggle the baby while moving my arms from side to side, gently tapping his butt in time to music—not like a spanking, just like a mullet-headed guy keeping time on his girlfriend's thigh while rocking out to Laser Floyd. This would quiet the baby and eventually induce sleep, especially if we put on industrial music or the "nuclear polka" of Brave Combo.

That was the good news about Dr. Sears. He reaffirmed our instincts when all the other "experts" were touting nursing schedules and crib training. Our kid was a screamer. He didn't sleep in his bassinet, and I didn't sleep in my bed. We slept together in a recliner, clinging to each other. Or else Jim would arrange five pillows into a pyramidal shape and prop the baby on his chest while I passed out on the couch for a few hours.

I wore the baby all day. I had slings and pouches and carriers. Striped ones. Floral ones. Black ones. Red tartan plaid ones. Ones with rings and ones with snaps and ones with buckles. Some had padding. Some did not. Outside the carrier, the baby would assume a pickle-sucking grimace and wail monotonously—including at night. Other people's babies rode around in travel systems and strollers; they lounged adorably on kitty blankets, nibbling on their toes. Mine was strapped to my chest like a suicide bomb for the first eight months. Well-intentioned acquaintances waggled their fingers invitingly, but when I unbuckled Baldo and handed him over, they would recoil from his squalling. Their bouncing methods and goofy faces proved futile.

According to Dr. Sears, this constant baby-wearing was not only benign—it was desirable, promoting bonding, facilitating cognitive development, and helping the baby and mother feel secure. It was all good.

But one statement stuck in my craw.

> Babywearing also prevents depression because a baby who is worn fusses less, so the mother feels more confident, less strained, and therefore less depressed.[17]

Dr. Sears goes on to state, "The goodness of a baby is not a measure of your effectiveness as a mother," but we've already stopped listening. We're back at "prevents depression."

The message of the attachment-parenting philosophy is clear: A satisfied baby doesn't cry. And a mother of an attached baby isn't depressed. Both statements are bullshit.

Yet mothers cling to them—as I did, initially—with almost religious fervor. All my friends, online and in real life, were Sears acolytes, and attachment parenting was working beautifully for them. Everyone got loads of sleep in the family bed, and their babies and toddlers were bright, inquisitive, roly-poly, and clear skinned. Their children did not vomit and scream.

And their babies *never cried*. One mother became indignant that babies were always said to cry in books and songs. Why, hers never did! What reason would a baby have to cry, unless he was strapped into an infant seat and ignored by his mother? Babies cried when they were abandoned in cribs and corked up with pacifiers. Haven't you read *The Continuum Concept?* Don't you know that among the Yequana tribe, children *never* cry? You're abusive!

These parents, of course, have empathetic and sensitive children whose every desirable characteristic is attributable to their having been carried in a sling for the first year, and they think "colic" is something that happens to horses.

I'd try to explain, acting out the tragedy of my son's gastrointestinal system with my fingers and hands. I'd pantomime nighttime itching and topical steroid application with my hands while I described my elimination diet. Still there'd be blank looks.

Desperate to get out of the house, I sweated through one playgroup meeting, unable to stop the crying. We nursed, rocked, bounced, checked diapers, changed diapers, chewed a teether, sipped water, and nursed some more before finally giving up after forty-five minutes of solid fussing. We carpooled home with a mother and her four-year-old, who kept asking, "Why is he crying? What's wrong with that baby?"

"His tummy is hurt," I'd said. "It's broken." I was white-knuckled at the wheel. I dropped them off at home and waved good-bye. We didn't hear from them again.

At a pool party, I met a nice couple whose six-month-old had just outgrown his colic. They still looked fearful, as if waiting for a sudden breeze or a loud noise to send him into neurological overdrive.

I approached the mother, who was joggling back and forth with the baby in a pouch-style sling while trying to talk to the host about his postdoctoral fellowship.

"Ah," I observed. "The sling dance. I recall it well."

She looked at me as if I'd been reading her mail.

"Does your son have colic?" I asked. "Mine did, too—well, reflux, actually."

"Really?" she asked. "What did you do?"

"Same thing you're doing now."

The mother sighed. "We went to Zilker Park," she explained, "to get out one day. And you know what these people we met said to us? 'I guess we just never gave our kids a *reason* to cry.' Can you believe that?"

Actually I could. The people she met were the *winners*. They got easy kids. They had, we assume, the financial and social wherewithal to parent them gently—with a breast rather than a pacifier or pumped milk, with a stay-at-home mother rather than a paid caregiver, with in-arms loving. They got the bragging rights. They got a return on their investment immediately. And they somehow won the right to judge everyone else.

They were happy and sane. If we were good mothers, we would be, too.

Nor is Dr. Sears's paternalistic advice about postpartum depression particularly helpful. In none of the four pages devoted to it in *The Baby Book* does he mention thoughts of suicide or self-harm, but condescending language does count "lack of interest in grooming and physical attractiveness, and a negative attitude toward husband" among the hallmarks of PPD. Sears's advice almost entirely comprises self-care measures that sound like a health brochure from the 1950s ("Practice good grooming" and "Stick to priorities" among them, as if depressed people are capable of that). Expert therapy merits a two-sentence mention; antidepressant medication, though considered compatible with breastfeeding in many cases, is not mentioned.

Nor is postpartum psychosis, a rare but serious and sudden-onset illness that requires *immediate* medical intervention and usually hospitalization, mentioned in the book. (Someone has since included a cursory discussion of it on Sears's official website.) In fact, Dr. Sears recommends a medical consultation only *after* the self-care measures have been tried and discourages mothers from receiving therapy that "would result in mother-baby separation." Tellingly, he places this information (along with the toll-free number for Depression After Delivery) in a section headlined "Tips for Dads."

So the book reminded me to brush my hair, share the bed, and "let baby be your therapist," but Dr. Sears didn't tell me what to do when I stopped sleeping and started cutting my hands with the baby's nail clippers. Not even a French pedicure could have stopped my fantasies of suicide, which were becoming awfully vivid.

Some of Sears's other advice to women is really tin-eared and unsympathetic. (We'll leave aside the matter that "his" books largely describe his *wife's* parenting techniques.) The asker of a hypothetical question in the "Nighttime Parenting" chapter of *The Baby Book* grouses that her two-year-old doesn't seem to nap, but "I need a break." The doctor's response is, of course, to "nap with her." "You probably look forward to her nap time so you can 'finally get something done.' Resist this temptation," he advises. Yet sometimes things *need* to get done—teeth brushed, mortgages paid, phone calls returned. Never mind that a mother may be depressed. Maybe she, a grown woman, just doesn't want to take a nap. I read this passage and felt crushed. I'm not going to be able to get anything done for *two years?* There seems to be no real awareness of the frustration primary caregivers feel.

I've also seen far too many mothers beat themselves silly about using pacifiers, swings, and other tools (what Dr. Sears calls "artificial baby soothers" or "mechanical mothers") with their babies. When I caught my mother trying to slip a Nuk into my screaming baby's mouth, I tried to throw her out of the house. We had a fight, and I fled to the parking lot of a liquor store, where I sat and cried and felt like a big piece of shit—despised by my family, unable to comfort my child, fighting the urge to drink kosher wine out of a bag.

Despite the occasional generic disclaimer ("Wherever all your family members sleep the best is the right arrangement for you"), the Sears formula is too rigid and dogmatic. *Especially* if you're a depressed and isolated mother. The first thing you lose when you are depressed is your recognition of qualitative difference. Every setback is a crisis; every uncertainty is the worst-case scenario. You are either a heroic attached mother with a content, satisfied baby or you are a failure. You are giving your child less than the best. You are compromising your baby's well-being if you can't sleep with her beside you or in the same room. You are compromising your baby's well-being if you are a single or working parent who relies upon childcare and bottle-feeding of breast milk or formula. (Naturally, Dr. Sears recommends nanny care at home if you "must" have paid caregiving, but he gives no explanation for this preference.) And if you are a depressed person who cannot provide your child the continuous loving interaction and homemade play pillows depicted in the Sears illustrations, you may feel that your very presence is a detriment to your child.

The Fussy Baby Book was closer to the mark but still off target. I liked the dastardly looking cover baby. A tiny, wicked Damien, lacking only a mustache to twirl and some cartoon TNT. Could the Searses have a sense of humor after all?

Ours was a variant of fussiness: the *hurting* baby, who screams due to unrelenting pain of a mysterious nature. We knew this, of course. We did not know how to stop the pain. Dr. Sears recommended an elimination diet, which we tried. Dr. Sears recommended anti reflux medications, which we also tried. And of course Dr. Sears recommended attachment parenting, which we had tried.

Worse, the parents quoted in *The Fussy Baby Book* were those stubborn Sears acolytes, those people who swore that their uncuddly, frantic infants were the most precious gifts they had ever received and they wouldn't have it any other way, even though they had been kicked out of childcare centers and banned from playdates.

Let's not bullshit ourselves, people. *Of course* you'd have it another way if you could. It's not your child's job to teach you the meaning of compassion. Your kid's job is to play and eat snacks and grow up to be independent from you. Your child does not suffer in order to build your character. If you could take all the reflux out of your child's body and put it into yours, you would. So don't shine me on about how you're thankful for your child's fussiness.

At the core of the Sears philosophy is the belief that children should be held and nurtured and made to feel safe and comfortable in the earliest stages of life so that they will not develop insecurities. They will grow into confident and empathetic adults. Naturally, no mother would disagree with this concept. Why, before Dr. Sears came around and put his brand on it, this idea belonged to women and was called *mothering*. Was Dr. Sears a necessary antidote to the Spocks of the world, the advocates of playpens and scheduled feedings and crying jags that "strengthened the lungs"? Quite possibly. But wouldn't it have been nicer to just renounce this paternalistic "expert" logic instead of replacing it with a kinder, gentler variety, one that didn't carry a designer label, like "the Brazelton method" or "a Sears baby"? (My child, for example, is very much an Ingman baby.) One that didn't quietly endorse the old, tired concept of the heroic, self-sacrificing mother?

One morning I took Baldo to a park one neighborhood over,

unaware that it was ground zero for Sears parenting in my town. They seemed like nice enough people, and their children were amusing little perspicacious homeschoolers who admired our sand castles and rattled off facts about Charlemagne. Soon the adult chatter around the playscape turned to commiseration over soy elimination and sleep talk.

"Do you know Linda?" one mother asked another. "Did you meet her at La Leche League? Well, anyway, she's got it worse than we do."

"Really?"

"If she moves at all, her five-year-old wakes up. And her three-year-old wakes up at 1 AM and *stays up.*"

A gasp of schadenfreude. *"Really?"*

"But fortunately, her mother lives in the same townhouse complex and is really understanding."

We left quietly. Was this a parenting style or an inculcation of female masochism, or both? Was someone going to win the Stella Dallas Memorial Award for Greatest Maternal Sacrifice, Sleep-Loss Division?

There's a certain type of parent I see often—sometimes I see it in myself—who is a success-oriented person from a middle-class background, well-taught (traditionally or through self-education) and accustomed to high praise. We're used to getting a report card or a performance review every six weeks, we're current with Big Ideas and prone to Big Discussions over pints of Guinness, and we throw ourselves into parenting with the same right-minded stamina with which we might compare graduate programs and scholarships.

We educate ourselves about various theoretical orientations on the topic, read the works of champion scholars (Barbara Coloroso, Penelope Leach, Dr. Jay Gordon), memorize acronyms and slogans, and align ourselves with a "good match." We study rigorously, and our parenting is like a practicum. We analyze situations and apply theories; we fasten Snappis and gently redirect toddlers with great self-satisfaction, as if we are strutting for a review committee. We meet over coffee with study groups.

This is not necessarily lamentable. It's good to be well read, to be prepared, to invest oneself in the new role of parent. It's just not really about the *kids*, is it? It's about more than just wanting to be good at what you do; it's about wanting to be *the best*. We're parenting careerists. We want to be superstars. We want other people to praise us. We want props for holding off on antibiotics for that ear infection, for delaying solids just a little longer, for buying the organic crib sheets and the shampoo that's made with kukui nuts harvested by the indigenous people of Brazil and imported by a woman-owned business. We go that one extra mile. We *exceed* expectations. If we were an airline, we'd be Lufthansa.

Is this wrong? Again, not necessarily. It's not wrong to have ambitions, to dream of home-sewn Halloween costumes (or ones we just "whipped up" because we're so crafty) and slow food and perfect portraits and cooperative preschool.

But we have to remember that our standards of success, of happiness, of demonstrating our love for our children are inflated. We'll never meet them. Our reach will always exceed our grasp. Some days it's perfectly legitimate to feel proud that everyone is simply still *alive*. It would have been a banner day for our ancient homonid ancestor, Java Man, if everyone came through it alive and more or less fed.

What the fuck does all this yuppie blather have to do with postpartum depression, you ask? Plenty, as it turns out. One of the criteria for measuring postpartum depression is the presence of feelings of maternal inadequacy. And if you're in the business of making mothers feel inadequate, you're compounding the problem.

Parents—especially mothers, for reasons of socialization as much as biology—who carry this great bilious load of unattainable expectations are punching a one-way ticket to Crazy Town. If our baby isn't content and approvingly silent, like a neonatal customer service supervisor, we have *failed*. It sounds risible on paper—of course we haven't *failed*—but when you're sleep deprived and suddenly isolated for long stretches of time, and you used to be the star system administrator in the networking team or you used to discuss Proust with your book group, you can quite literally go fucking insane. Now, I'm not suggesting that parenting is a stultifying task. The difference is that no one else is around to stroke your ego. Isn't that what we crave?

And there's a considerable difference between *endorsing* certain parenting techniques (such as breastfeeding or the family bed) and *prescribing* what turns out to be, in essence, a regimen for living. If you're going to wear a sling, why not wear an organic one? If you're going to wear an organic sling, why not wear one hand-sewn by a work-at-home mom? If you're going to wear an organic sling hand-sewn by a work-at-home mom, make sure you feed your little one organic squash. And delay vaccinations. Use cloth diapers—organic hemp ones, of course—or elimination communication. Avoid plastic toys; use simple toys made of natural materials.

There's nothing wrong with any of these decisions. But can you really do it all? Assuming you can even afford organic produce and WAHM diapers (which is a classist assumption in itself), is it really the end of the road for your kid if you bring home a trash bag full of motley hand-me-down Legos instead of a Waldorf doll? If you use sanitized thrift-store throw pillows instead of the homemade cylindrical bolsters Dr. Sears suggests? Aren't you entitled to make these sorts of decisions individually? To pick and choose? To feel good about *some* of your accomplishments, even if you don't have a perfect score?

When you are depressed, you reach a point when you cease to be a rational being making a series of decisions; rather, you fluctuate violently between Success and Failure at every turn. Every moment is literally either a victory or a crisis. You are understimulating your child or smothering her. You are feeding her hazardous pesticides. That Infant Tylenol and Motrin might be destroying her liver. And so you are locked in a cycle of anxiety, which feeds your depression, which impairs your ability to cope, which increases your certainty that you are the shittiest person alive.

You must be, since you're wearing the baby and you're still depressed.

Attachment parenting has its uses, certainly. If you choose to sleep in a bed with your baby, it's good to have solid medical backing against the claim that you are sure to smother her or give her SIDS.

(Does it follow that you are harming her if you choose otherwise? Not necessarily.) And I've seen anticonsumerist feminists argue quite cogently that attachment parenting practices comprise a rejection of the "baby-industrial complex"—the stockpiles of wipe warmers, "Mommy bears," upmarket strollers, crib bedding, and other nonsense pitched as necessities to expectant parents. The message that a mother needs only her breasts and her arms to raise a child is indubitably strong. Still, we must be careful not to allow her only her breasts and her arms. Don't deny her a swing or a bouncer or a fellow caregiver or real help if she's losing her mind.

Finally, my search for like-minded people led me back to the Internet.

I wrote to an expat friend I had made in Finland, a lesbian mother of fraternal twins. She had put one baby down screaming in order to diaper the other. She stopped breastfeeding. She was a no-bullshit lady.

I wrote to her:

> *I was reading* The Fussy Baby Book, *and the stories in the back are so "Madison had horrible colic and reflux and ear infections, and she screamed for seven months, and even now at age four she'll burst into tears if a door slams and only sleeps if I place her facing north-northwest on a bamboo mat with a blue sock on and a red sock on, but I wouldn't trade my high-need baby for anything in the world! Once I adjusted my attitude, I realized I had been given a precious gift!" Uhh . . . what? That's great for you, if you feel that way, but I don't think I'm on that bus. I think I'm on the bus with the crazy postpartum chicks.*

She wrote back with some wonderful advice: *Put Dr. Sears down. Step away from The Book. No one will ever live up to the Holy Sainted Madonna Stepford Wife Martha, so don't even try. And then get the hell out of Dodge for a few hours.*

I did.

CRYING IT OUT

I'D ABOUT DECIDED that Dr. William Sears could kiss my sweet Texas ass.

Why, then, was I gleeful to discover a sleep book endorsed by the man? Elizabeth Pantley's *No-Cry Sleep Solution* promised "gentle ways to help your baby sleep through the night." It was perfect. Except for one thing: It didn't work for us.

We kept logs of "naptime" and "night," stretches of time virtually indistinguishable from "waking" and "daytime." By now Baldo was waking up tearfully every forty-five minutes to nurse at night. One of our "logs" from this experiment bears the legend FUCK THIS, written in a childlike scrawl neither of us recognizes as our own hand. I was sobbing all day and all night. It was about this time that I tried to kill myself but couldn't get anyone to watch Baldo. Pantley's Gentle Removal Plan—you sneak the baby off your nipple and out of your arms—fell flat for us. I'd count to one hundred, begin easing my nipple out of Baldo's mouth, and then break into tears when he screamed and awoke. We couldn't get him out of our arms. He wouldn't even sleep beside us. He wanted to sleep on my chest or on Jim's. I can't sleep all night on my back with a baby on top of me.

At the end of her book, Pantley admits "Not every mommy I worked with had fabulous, immediate success. A few parents struggled for weeks until they felt it was completely hopeless." She goes on to add, "If you are at this point in *your* life [emphasis original], I'm going to give you three ideas that are drastically different from anything else I have suggested. You are obviously at a dangerous level of extreme emotions, and you don't want to accidentally hurt your baby in the night by shaking her or hitting her." And then Pantley goes on to recommend the "old" advice of putting your baby in her crib and letting her cry—the measures you were trying to avoid by buying her book! But her word choice makes clear: This is not because *the plan* has failed—this is because *you* are out of control. *You* have failed, and *you* might hurt the baby. Again, there's no recognition that sleeplessness is harmful to mothers or parents, aside from impairing their caregiving abilities. ("Of course, by now *you* may be on a cocktail of psychiatric medicines and fantasizing about suicide while you secretly mutilate yourself, but don't worry! It's much more important that the baby *never cries!*")

So then it was on to Marc Weissbluth, M.D., author of the promisingly titled *Healthy Sleep Habits, Happy Child* and founder of the Sleep Disorders Center at Children's Memorial Hospital in Chicago. I'd heard raves from mothers I trusted about his sleep-training program. And these were not Mothers Who Are Not Like Us, those mysterious creatures who think snacks are "spoiling" and organized religion wild and permissive. One was an urban goth mom with multicolored ponyfalls, and the other was a freaky rock chick who'd drunk absinthe in New Orleans with GWAR. The first person to congratulate her on her pregnancy had been Jerry Only of The Misfits. Another was my friend living in Finland with her wife and twin babies. These were not parenting-magazine sheep. These were bright and creative people who loved their children, who'd read the "right" books and tried the "right" methods, and simply needed a different answer.

After four hours of rocking, nursing, and driving one night, I freaked out and took the 183 flyover to A Corporate Mega-Bookstore on the side of the highway. There I found a copy of the Weissbluth tome, a darling, rosy-cheeked infant asleep with a teddy bear on its cover. The jacket blurb promised a "step-by-step regimen for instituting beneficial habits within the framework of your child's natural sleep cycles." What could be better?

As the prologue suggested, I resisted the temptation to skip ahead to the regimen and instead read the first chapter—which turned out to be a harrowing jeremiad about "fatigued, fussy brats" who were "more likely to become fat kids." (God forbid! Fat!) *The sleep they miss is gone forever*, Weissbluth warned. Cumulative sleep losses would ruin my child's life. Children with longer sleep patterns score higher than others on reading and vocabulary tests. There is a correlation between sleep disturbances and attention-deficit hyperactivity disorder (ADHD). Children who sleep poorly are more subject to injuries during the day. At no point does Weissbluth claim that sleepless children are more likely to spontaneously combust, but I would have believed it.

I threw the book across the room when I read that night waking is "not caused" by teething or gastroesophageal reflux. Of course, meticulous studies bear out his assertions, but how could I forget my child's grunting, fitful nights, his twisting and tossing and awakening in a puddle of vomit? At least Weissbluth conceded that the itching of atopic dermatitis could cause sleep disturbance. Moreover, he theorized that "colic" babies—or I guess what Dr. Sears would call a "hurting" baby—become accustomed to the soothing we provide and are unable to regulate themselves without it as they grow older.

All this information eventually led up to the "step-by-step plan," which is curiously difficult to actually locate in the book. It involves a rigorous schedule of daytime and nighttime sleep—always in the child's bed or crib. Parents are to place the child in his or her sleeping place after a brief transitional ritual and leave the room, locking the door or using a crib tent if necessary. Not for nothing is this man known as the "nap Nazi." His *Sturmabteilung* are the zealous parents whose anecdotes pepper the book. Like the Sears acolytes, they espouse an all-or-nothing approach to parenting technique. By following the plan to the letter, they transformed their overtired, wired children into "angels": cheerful, affectionate, well-adjusted.

One mother expresses particular scorn for the attachment ilk:

> I am aware that the practice of toting your baby along with you on every occasion is the new social thing. No doubt it stems from the "me" generation that a baby should not be allowed to interfere with your lifestyle. So parents everywhere are seen with their infants: in grocery stores, restaurants, the homes of friends.[18]

Babies in grocery stores? How shocking. These narcissistic parents probably want to buy cereal or something. Remind me not to mention the time we took the baby to my editor's fiftieth birthday party, where there was a noisy band and a giant buffet, and where I stuffed my face for hours with the baby in a sling while the honoree's delightful elderly parents enthused about how mothers don't have to be stuck at home anymore. Oops, I just did.

If you follow the Weissbluth infant plan with two naps a day, you will not leave the house. If you go to the park to push the baby on a swing and chat with other parents, you will leave after forty-five minutes. Your child will be adequately rested, but you will be batshit. If you are already batshit, you will be more batshit. The only adult voice you will hear will belong to Montel. This is not an answer.

Neither parenting plan is flexible enough to make room for the needs or personality of an individual parent. If you allow for spontaneity, will your kid be a "raging beast"? If you impose a structure, will your child be "unconnected": emotionally insecure, neurologically disorganized? Each camp blames the other for ADHD, so your child is virtually guaranteed to have it, no matter which you choose.

Here's another thing Sears and Weissbluth have in common: the logic that if you don't buy the book and practice the method, your child is totally, irrevocably fucked into adolescence and beyond.

I hate this approach, especially when it's coming at me from men. Go ahead and call me a dour, braless feminist; I am, so you'd be right. For millennia, women have mothered and men have fathered without expert commentary. There are no parenting magazines in rural Lapland, yet people grow and thrive there and tend reindeer. This does not mean we should publish a best-selling manual advising young parents to mimic the Lapps. All we really need is a way to collect information—from doctors, from our children, from other parents—and enough confidence to weigh our options and cast out those that don't suit us.

To wit, I decided that I was no longer going to crash on the couch and trade off four-hour shifts with Jim all night, walking and rocking our almost-year-old baby. I did not accept as destiny my son's waking every forty-five minutes, wanting to nurse. Neither did I accept as destiny my sequestration in our domicile. Mothers and babies are meant to meet other mothers and babies, not to be cordoned off in little pairs and hidden behind walls. We are meant to share resources—opinions, stories, food, supervision, clothing, toys, books. Yet I wanted to instill a sense of regularity in our lives—not a routine, but a rhythm, a flow from the beginning of the day to its end. And fuck if I was going to stick my kid in a crib, close the door, and leave him all night long until he accepted his solitude.

We needed a plan. A good plan. A gradual plan. A thoughtful plan. But a *plan*, dammit.

We stayed with attachment parenting until the reflux subsided—which it did, to my estimable delight—around eight months, when Baldo could finally sit up. I'd been sure that he'd be one of the tiny number of kids who keep on having reflux, who sleep on inclined pillows and have fundoplication surgery and take Tagamet at snacktime. I was sure that he'd grow up to vomit on his dinner companions. But it stopped. You could have knocked me over with a burp cloth. And for that I was grateful. I was grateful that no one had made me feel guilty about holding my child or wearing him in a carrier. I was grateful that there was support from somewhere inside the medical community for clutching my kid and shuffling around the room while he screamed into my ear, for putting him in the bed with us at night, instead of leaving him to wail.

But it wasn't enough. He still didn't sleep.

We stumbled onto a night-weaning program endorsed by Dr. Jay Gordon, an attachment-friendly pediatrician. *Not until the baby is a year old*, he warned. Baldo was eleven months. Close enough. Our interpretation of Dr. Gordon's advice consisted of the following regimen: Nurse and rock baby until sleeping. Hand to Jim, who is waiting in bed, propped up on phalanx of pillows. Put in earplugs. Go out to couch. Sleep until morning. It was heaven. After about a week of it, I actually felt slightly restored mentally. My obsessive thoughts about death slowed. I didn't cry all day. Jim did all the nighttime comforting.

The idea is that the night waking will curtail when the baby realizes nursing is no longer available. That didn't happen, either. Instead, Jim had a nervous breakdown from shuffling the baby all night and teaching twelve-year-olds all day. He traded in his car for a Jeep, threatened to divorce me, and began fantasizing about vehicular suicide. (It was my idea first.) "I haven't been happy once since this baby was born," he wept. Enter the psychiatrist and the Paxil.

So at last we capitulated and embarked upon a modified Weissbluth regimen. Those of you who are without sleep for fifteen months may cast the first stone. We decided that saying goodnight and closing the door until morning was too harsh for us. But it was time for Baldo to learn to sleep.

We prepared as if planning an invasion. I made a book entitled

My Bed. Laminated it at Kinko's. Read it to Baldo every day for two weeks. "My bed is a quiet place," I read, pointing at a picture—stolen from the web—of someone's six-month-old sleeping peacefully. "I am safe in my bed." We rolled the crib next to our bed and took the gate off so Baldo could climb into it and play. I lay inside it too.

Then the day came at last. In my journal, I wrote:

> *Tonight is the night we've been waiting for.*
>
> *Our baby has slept on every imaginable surface. The car seat. The couch. A duffle bag on top of the dryer. A recliner. Now it's time for him to sleep in his crib on his own.*
>
> *For me it's like putting the baby in a claw trap and leaving him out as bear bait. I've heard too much negative press. It's a "baby prison." He'll shake the bars and rattle his sippy cup. American mothers are horrible for leaving their tiny children down the hall in little cages with cute bumpers that match the window valances instead of snuggling with them in a cozy family bed with Mexican blankets full of pet fur. Hence our babies grow up to be neurotics on Paxil, just like we are. Crying it out is abuse.*
>
> *But I'm not going to lie: I'm excited in a way. It has been a month of Sundays since I slept in my own bed all night, adjacent to my life partner. I won't have to stumble from one end of the house to the other to go to the bathroom in the middle of the night. I can actually get dressed in the same room where I keep my clothes instead of streaking through the house every morning, avoiding the picture window. Okay, maybe I'll still streak through the house every morning.*

Yet we were nervous, so I stockpiled supplies to get us through the next week. I set aside a bottle of Rescue Remedy. Two pairs of silicone earplugs. Our CD of *The Downward Spiral*. My VHS tape of *Tetsuo: The Iron Man*. I charged the cordless phone so I could go outside and call a mama friend who'd agreed to step us through it. She did CIO and survived.

I realized I didn't have enough crib sheets. We'd had the same one on the babyless crib since we set it up a year ago. I'd need extras in case the baby vomited from crying, a prospect that nauseated me yet was likely, according to the books. Likewise, our mama buddy advised that we have alcohol on hand. Not that we wanted to be drunkenly incapacitated. I had half a jug of Chilean red on hand; it tasted like bell peppers, and I wasn't looking forward to that.

We went to the Infant Superstore. The bedding really got me. It was adorable. I had such scorn for this stuff, but as it turns out, I am not made of stone after all. There was a set with a baby Snoopy on it, looking as he must have when Charlie Brown picked him out at the Daisy Hill Puppy Farm. All the selections had a mien of gentleness, of tender and soft things to surround and comfort a tiny child. Platitudinous rhetorical questions ran through my mind: *When do we lose our innocence? Why not decorate our children's rooms with tiny baby office cubicles and little televisions?* I'm not a particularly imaginative depressive. I'm just a mother, and I get misty in spite of myself.

Another mother rolled her cart up to mine and said hello. By then, I was sniffling and snuffling, and Baldo was gnawing a hole in the cardboard box for a training bowl. She asked me the usual baby questions to start a conversation: "How old is yours?" "Oh, mine is seventeen months. I like this age." Her son also had reflux. She lived in Oak Hill. We chatted back and forth. Her name was Mona. I liked her. We stopped short of exchanging numbers, which I would later regret, but our kids "said goodbye" to each other, which is, of course, conversational shorthand for shy parents. I didn't see her again in the store, but I imagined her driving back to Oak Hill with her training bowl and her wallpaper borders or whatever it was she bought, and I felt as if everything was going to be okay somehow. We'd all be okay if we just kept going forward and doing our best.

I stopped at the natural-foods grocery store a block away. I got a bottle of vino verde and a shiraz, my favorite wines, even though I think Jim had in mind for me to stop off at the Gas 'n Sip for a suitcase of Schlitz. I picked through the herbals and homeopathics the way I always did, as if I was going to find a natural, wholesome, and quick-dissolving remedy for Infant Weltschmerz or for Anxious Personhood. There's a secret ingredient somewhere, some weed with yellow flowers, that we can dry and grind up into a capsule to make the hard choices easier. It costs a lot, but you only have to use a little and it smells good. Instead I added to our cart a bottle of Delirium Nocturnum, a Belgian novelty ale with a pink elephant stumbling around on the label. The pies weren't promising, so I picked out two spelt doughnuts, one for each of us to have after dinner. Unfortunately, I ate both of them after lunch.

And then we did it.

We laid him down in his bed and told him that we loved him. We sang him two songs. We told him it was time to sleep, just as Elizabeth Pantley recommends in the last part of her book. We rubbed his back and told him goodnight. We returned in five-minute intervals to reassure him that we were still here and that he was safe.

I'm still known among my immediate circle of friends as "the mom who cried it out." None of my friends had postpartum depression and babies with reflux. So what can I say?

THE GOOD **THERAPIST**

DR. S. LIKES MANDARIN COLLARS and flowy fabrics, jewel tones, straight-legged pants. Her voice is a half-whisper, full of air. We meet in a commercial park across the freeway from my house, the kind with a sandstone facade and a lofty-sounding name that suggests professional élan and harmony with nature—it's carved into a hilly, environmentally sensitive part of town overrun with McMansions and chichi boutiques. We are getting somewhere, even though I tighten inside at her lexicon: *karma, cognitive restructuring, being your word*. She makes frequent reference to *The Road Less Traveled*, and she's asked me repeatedly if I believe in God. I'm a little scared.

I've had psychoanalysis before. My first shrink was a buxom child psychiatrist with a too-tight Toni home perm and peasant blouses with concho belts. I was four. I'd been sleeping poorly and frightening myself with my own imaginings. We played cards throughout every session; I can't fathom the clinical significance of Go Fish. I returned to her after my sister died.

Dr. E. asked me to tell her how I felt about my sister's death, and I didn't want to. I left the room and hid out in the bathroom until our session was over. I wanted to be a regular fifth-grade kid. I didn't want people to be awkward around me. I didn't want to have to get special permission to read *A Taste of Blackberries*, our class's book selection, about a kid whose best friend dies from a bee-sting allergy. It wouldn't have mattered if I hadn't read the book at all; the teacher never asked me questions or called on me to talk about it. Maybe things are different now, but in our class we just learned "about" things that existed independently from us in a discrete, empirical fashion: the planets and their moons, the Underground Railroad, fractions. Death was for puppies and the occasional grandparent.

I went back to analysis willingly the first time I went crazy. Jim and I had been married for a couple of years. We were living in California and I was clinging to my first real writing job. I was part of a team of writers for a trade publisher; our first office was down the hall from the industry-standard catalog for the hardware business. As a group, we would change hands three times in three years, traded between corporate entities like a box of staplers. A lawsuit here, a buyout there, a layoff here, a hiring there, an IPO here, a restructuring there, until finally everyone was bankrupt and we were all out of work. Meanwhile, Jim had flung himself into the workforce with the vigor of a stunned cow in a slaughterhouse and spent most days prostrate on the couch, trying to win radio call-in contests.

Subsequently, my head became full of irrational notions. I had fibromyalgia. I was pregnant. I was infertile. I had mercury poisoning from my fillings. I could eat no carbohydrates, only peanut butter and bacon. I dropped below my high school weight from ketosis, and my kidneys almost failed. Twice, I ended up in the ER with vague but alarming symptoms—thrombosis? Appendicitis? I stopped sleeping at night. I'd sit, hollow eyed, on our couch, watching infomercials and obscure late-night talk shows with unrecognizable hosts and guests dredged from the sociocultural peat bog surrounding greater Los Angeles. As I, twitching and tense, watched a short-haired, sober C. C. DeVille perform with his new speed-metal band, I knew I needed help.

My doctor rifled through my file, prescribed Xanax, then Serzone, then Prozac, then Doxepin. The Serzone didn't help. It gave me tremors in my legs instead. I quit Serzone cold turkey over Memorial Day weekend at a bed and breakfast in the Texas Hill Country. I clung to the threadbare couch in the living room all night, convinced that I was actually on the ceiling. I started Prozac, and it was a miracle. Within the first week, I surprised myself by singing while I was cooking—something I always did when I was well. I wasn't crying anymore. I could lie down and eventually go to sleep at night. I flourished, until I eventually broke out in hives from the medicine.

The doctor also recommended therapy. Off I went to see P., a licensed therapist who wore t-shirts puff-painted with humpback whales and played ambient rain-forest white noise in her waiting room. She had me play out my suicidal fantasies in my mind; I'd swallow my stash of Ultram with a bottle of Wild Turkey, and the world would close up into darkness, like an iris shot from a D. W. Griffith movie. No longer hobbled by a crazy, hypochondriacal spouse, Jim would become motivated and fabulously successful. My family would be angry that I had failed in my task—to be the good kid, the surviving kid, the kid nobody had to worry about—but they would forgive me. P. gave me relaxation tapes and taught me diaphragmatic breathing techniques. Then she retired from private practice.

I don't know if it helped, but once my corporate masters freed me from my state of literary serfdom and I slid into an undemanding editorial job, I felt better. I'd surf the web at lunch and walk down to the corner for enchiladas. We paid the rent. My biggest worry was getting pegged by a golf ball from the municipal course across the street; errant Top Flites were always bashing windows and denting cars.

I got so cocky that Jim and I bought a house. We got a cat. We stopped using birth control. I became pregnant immediately, which eventually brought me to Dr. S.

At one point, Dr. S. tells me that her babies are dead. One was stillborn; the other lived nine days. She had a hysterectomy thereafter, then a divorce.

Another time, she tells me that the most significant predictor of adolescent depression isn't the parents' divorce, poverty, or even the death of a parent. It is, she says, the death of a sibling.

One of the themes of our work together is that I am overly judgmental and cynical. "Snippy," she says at one point. At first I am loath to accept this assessment of my personality. Then I decide to step back and consider it for a while.

I am an editor. Fault-finding is my stock-in-trade. Moreover, I do have a stick up my ass. I feel personally offended by every comma splice I encounter, every heading typeset in the wrong case. Every mistake executed around me confirms my grammatical and general superiority to others. Editors make unforgiving lovers.

I decide to accept Dr. S.'s conclusion. But in my odd moments I will wonder if I'm not submitting to some kind of masochistic ego-abrasion, the kind Dr. Laura Schlessinger dispenses. God, I hope that's not what's happening.

During one session, Dr. S. credits a Landmark Education Forum with allowing her to get herself back together after her children died and her marriage fell apart. She encourages me to attend a forum. I am frightened as I drive home. But because I don't wish to be judgmental and cynical, I make a deal with myself that I'll look into it. I've never heard of this thing before. When I do look into it, I am positively terrified. I do not want to cast aspersions upon any process that allows a grieving mother to feel relief and embrace her life after such a tragedy. But the thought of assembling in an office park and being browbeaten does not appeal to me. Paying $400 for the privilege appeals to me even less.

To drive home the point, my friend A. calls from Seattle. "Get out," she says. Not *hello*. "Get out. It's a cult. Get out." It turns out A. has been to a session of the Landmark Forum. They're good, she says. They'll mess up your head and you won't even know it. I also hear that they are rather litigious, so I will take pains to point out that these remarks are strictly the opinion of my friend A.

Then I make a second deal with myself. I will remember that psychotherapy is a tool that I am holding in my hand, like an awl (which is funny considering that I've never held an awl in my life, actually). I will not forget that I am the operator of this tool, not its object. I will put down my awl if it ceases to be useful. Dr. S. is only a person in a chair, sitting across from me and giving me her opinions. I am no less a person in a chair, sitting across from her and having my opinions. I will be open to the suggestions Dr. S. makes. I will respect her intelligence and her insight. But I will remember that my ideas are my own. I will terminate our relationship if I feel uncomfortable.

I will not commit to additional treatment measures unless I deem them necessary. And I will trust myself to determine what is right for me. If I am strong enough to be here, if I am strong enough to talk to a stranger about hurting myself and wanting to abandon my family, then I am strong enough to make my own decisions about my recovery.

In so many ways, I feel that her provocative remarks are spot on. She tells me that I am angry at Jim about something. My anger is part of the very foundation of our relationship. I consider it and can see her point. I realize that I very often am pissed off, unjustifiably, at Jim. What for? For not being me? When I agree with Dr. S., she tells me I am "coachable." Something in my gut twinges; does she mean malleable? Suggestible? I can only determine what that word means for me. It means that I am open to new ways of thinking. It means that I am well enough to go to her office and listen and decide for myself.

If I am well enough to do that, then maybe I am well. Enough.

I am confident enough in our therapeutic relationship to return to her office one more time. We are preparing for our first trip with the baby, a visit to California. I am nervous about the flight, about staying in hotel rooms, about conducting the interview I have scheduled, about seeing all of Jim's family. I am anxious about schlepping a stroller and a car seat through the security screenings. I am anxious about getting sunburned or motion sick. I am afraid of stepping on something sharp, worried that we'll be in a room next to a guest with a wet, hacking cough, like the person who kept me awake all night one time when I was staying for business at the Trump Taj Mahal. I am worried about meteors speeding toward the Earth's atmosphere and cratering LAX while I am standing at the baggage claim. I am not in good shape.

It's back to the office park, back to the chair across from Dr. S.'s couch.

I realize that I'm putting lots of effort into framing my remarks, lest I displease her. Smiling a lot. I'd wanted an ass-kicking therapist, but I'd also wanted the opportunity to unplug my polite conversational mechanisms and communicate from my emotional baseline. I want to be able to rant. As I think this, I also recognize there is value is reining myself in; I am learning to exercise control over my own perceptions. That's good, as long as it is I who is exercising control. To an extent I can't be sure if that's what's really happening.

I want to describe the feelings I had when I was living in California, the feelings that are haunting me now. The powerless feeling of being bought and sold at work. The feeling of having to prove my intelligence and worth in every conversation. The feeling of being mistaken for an employee and asked to provide service whenever I entered a retail establishment. The feeling of being stuck in traffic and debt. The feeling of being unable to walk anywhere. The feeling of having fighter jets from Miramar rip past my windows in twelve-minute intervals, firing their afterburners and shaking the walls. If I were still there, I'd probably be stuck in my depression forever. It's just really not the place for me to be.

"I have lots of negative associations," I finally say.

Dr. S. tells me these are feelings, not facts. I should suspend my judgments and assessments and think of myself as an anthropologist in a strange land. That's fair enough.

But what do you do, I ask her, when someone is trying to get under your skin with regard to something you feel strongly about? I am not thinking specifically of the trip now; I am extending her nonjudgmental logic to its extreme. What if someone is insulting you? At what point do you tell someone to shut the fuck up?

We don't. We refuse to be insulted. "I don't enroll in that," she asserts.

I twitch whenever I hear Landmark jargon, but I breathe deeply and let the idea sink in. I am smiling and seeing the light. I am bothered by the abuses visited on the innocent word "enroll," but this is useful. This is still okay. Not a problem. Not a problem at all. She gives me several examples of her nonenrollment in action with difficult people. Her strength and benevolence. Not a problem.

Now I feel comfortable enough to confess my unease with the demimonde of Southern California, to describe myself by contrast to it. Jim's parents are retired from prestigious and lucrative careers, whereas mine are farmers of hay. They golf and drive an SUV. They prepare sumptuous meals of osso buco from the *Reagan Family Cookbook*, whereas we barbecue brisket.

Dr. S. appears to be smirking. Am I judging too much?

"Well, see, it's just very different from what I was raised with."

Her smirk widens. "I see. And you say Jim is an only child?"

"Yes. As am I." I'm not quite sure I get what she's after.

"And so you stand to gain quite a bit, financially, by being married to him." Now her arms are folded.

The room is silent for a few moments. Is she calling me a gold-digger? And I'm not supposed to get angry?

Actually, I'm not angry, because she's just plain wrong. I could point out that I paid off Jim's student loans when we finished grad school and started living together, that I provided the full-time income and health insurance during the first years of our marriage, that for all she knows my parents could be eccentric billionaires who just like Schlitz and farming and brisket. That she's way the fuck out of line making rude personal pronouncements about a client's motivations for marriage. But who cares? She's already made up her mind.

Besides, our hour is almost over.

"It's too bad you're leaving tomorrow, because I think the Landmark seminar would be really valuable for you," she adds, gathering her notes.

"Yes, that's too bad."

"Maybe you'll be able to make it next time?"

"I just really don't think it's for me." I smile benignly, beginning to rise.

She stops on a dime. "Oh, you don't? Why would you think that?"

She's already told me that money shouldn't be a problem—not unless I undervalue my mental health, which I clearly don't, since

I'm here in her office paying $120 a session on my Visa. And I could bring my breast pump to collect milk for the baby during the day-long sessions.

"I think it's more, uh, intensive, than what I'm looking for." Is that nonjudgmental enough?

"How can you be sure of that?" she asks. "You don't know anything about the program."

Actually, I do. But not from the official sources.

I smile and shrug a little. "I just think an experience that intense is not for me, not right now."

Her hands find her hips. "How *dare* you?"

"I beg your pardon?"

"How *dare* you make assumptions about something you know nothing about? I'm really surprised at you, Marrit. You seemed so sensible." Funny, she's not acting very nonjudgmental all of a sudden. It seems like she gets to tell me everything she thinks or feels, and I have to sit there and smile and take it for the gospel. How is that therapeutic?

"Well, I'm sorry you feel that way."

She shakes her head. "I am so disappointed. I mean, how *dare* you?"

She's still glaring at me as she runs my credit card and gives me the slip to sign. "Anyway," she says, "shall we schedule our next session?"

"I'll, uh, need to give you a call once I'm back in town. Otherwise, I'll forget our appointment, I'm afraid."

Smiles are exchanged. The parking lot is sticky with the July heat. I giggle all the way home, and I don't go back. In fact, I don't go back to therapy at all.

About a year later, I see The Good Therapist at a coffee shop in my neighborhood. In a business suit, she is conversing with a guy in jacket and tie. There's a laptop folded in front of them. I breeze right through to the register and order my favorite coffee drink. Baldo has just started preschool, and I am celebrating our newest milestone. I have a contract for my book. We've even found a regimen for controlling his eczema. I am happy. I am wearing a crappy t-shirt and cutoffs; it's July in Texas, so who gives a shit? I sit on the back patio and smoke a cigarette. I'm reading *Writer's Digest*. More to the point, I feel very much like myself. I've stopped feeling like I'm interviewing for a job all the time, as if I need everyone's approval for how I conduct my life. How I parent my child. How I enjoy my relationships with people. I am not overly satisfied; I'm not smug, I'm not docile, I'm still angry about the things in life that rile me. I'm balanced. I'm ever so Marrity at last.

I am closer than ever to reaching the coveted state of being my dad describes as "doesn't give a shit." Within my family, this is an exalted state. You cannot honor anyone more highly than to say she *doesn't give a shit*. You are secure in yourself, pleased with what you have. You don't need anyone else's affirmation.

The best part about not giving a shit is that you don't have to wear it on your sleeve. Give a shit about not giving a shit? Never.

"Bye," I say to The Good Therapist as I leave.

WE'RE IN THIS **TOGETHER**

I HATE MY HUSBAND.

I hate his stupid USB hub, which flakes out whenever Windows crashes (often), so I have to go digging around behind the computer and unhook the scanner and scramble around for another port. It never happens to him, and I can't reproduce the problem. I can't remember what I was doing right before it crashed, because I was furious from the argument we were having and stuck on everything I wish I'd said, things that are more hurtful, more sarcastic, more acerbic.

I hate the way he tells me to put in my earplugs and let him handle it when the baby is crying, and then he tries to hold a conversation with me from across the room.

"I can't talk to you when you have those things in," he complains. I pull them out and throw them at him.

I hate the way his reassurances sound like indictments: "You just need to relax. You have to go to therapy. You just need to take a break." They could be rephrased slightly to be gentler.

"Nobody said those things to me when I was growing up," Jim says. I feel sorry for him, but he's a thirty-three-year-old man. Must I educate him constantly? Why does every conversation about my problems turn into a discussion of how he can't handle them? *Of course you can handle me, honey. You're a great guy! Let me help you!*

We have been together nine years at this point. None of these conversations are new. But having a baby amplified them. If our fights before were intimate, acoustic club shows, now they are stadium sellouts with pyrotechnic explosions and fountains of blood. We live together in a sleeper coach that rolls through the lulls toward its next destination, another knock-down in which we'll display our professional wordsmithery: *Fuck you! No, fuck you!*

Sometimes one or the other of us will threaten to leave. Yet we never have, not yet. Jim is a physical fighter, like a lot of men. He wears all of his emotions on his face. He's turned over our coffee table, punched walls. During our last fracas, mere minutes ago, he clenched up his fists and stood for a couple of moments in stock silence. I knew what this was.

"You want to hit me? Go ahead and do it!"

I'm a mean fighter, probably because I'm so small. I wouldn't ever want to get in a fight with myself. I am horribly insulting and I'll say anything. I've picked verbal arguments with people of every size and temperament. It's a wonder I haven't gotten my ass kicked. When I was scared and full of self-hate about motherhood, I dared Jim to leave.

On our worst day, I pulled from my bag of tricks what I imagined to be the worst slur against Jim's manhood. "You're horrible in bed."

He tried to reciprocate with an insult. "Well, you're a fucking hypocrite!" he opined.

"No, I'm not." That was that. You can call me a lot of things—like a crazy postpartum cunt—but I'm not hypocritical about it.

"That was all I could come up with," he admitted.

Nora Ephron has said that a baby is like a hand grenade thrown into a marriage. She's absolutely right. Though maybe it's more like a dirty bomb. I've heard people say that parenthood will fix their relationships, will make their women nurturing and their men faithful. That's the biggest fucking lie in the whole world. Having a baby will push your relationship to the very end of its elasticity. You will discover your limits as a person, possibly for the first time in your life. You will be happier than you've ever felt; you will be angrier than you've ever been.

If your experience is like mine, you will discover the point where compassion runs out, where you have no faith left and you want to turn and run or end it. I have never cried so much in my life. I have never wanted so desperately to drop something large and heavy on my husband with a forklift, not even when he gave his real, actual number to some drunk chick right in front of me while we were dating, not even when he blew off my rejections from graduate school. "God, are you still upset about that?" he asked a week after I got the last letter, his Southern California uptalk grating on my synapses. I wanted to throw him in front of a train. As it happens, we were at a subway stop in Boston at the time. I could have murdered Jim with the Green Line B train and been home in ten minutes.

And I'll tell you something else: The only thing worse than a baby is a *crying* baby. If your kid has colic or is fussy, your relationship is in for it. I've never been in combat, but I quite seriously imagine that it compares to the experience of being trapped in a house with your lover, your screaming baby, and yourself. There is literally no peace, day or night. The stress is absolutely unrelenting. Every minute leads only to another minute—another minute of pacing the floor, administering remedies that fail, wiping up puke, crying, hating yourself, being unable to sleep or eat.

The weird thing about becoming a parent with a partner is that you go through all this shit, you have these horrible fights that spiral out of control, and you want to keep your mouth shut, but you can't; you have to make one more hurtful comment, you have to push one more button, you have to twist the knife and rip and tear and cause just a little more pain before you'll be satisfied. But when it's over, you're both still there. You exchange looks full of meaning: *Wow, all that and the smoke cleared and we're both still here.* You are the most tenacious motherfuckers on goddamn planet Earth. You are the parenting equivalent of Legionnaires. When all this is over, you will get French citizenship and a comfortable pension. You are so badass, you deserve your own blaxploitation theme song that plays when you walk down the street.

You see happy people with easy lives, and you literally laugh at them. They're not even in your class. The stuff you used to complain about is a joke. What, a meeting went long and you had to hurry up to eat your sandwich? Get outta here. Your car was in the shop? Yeah, well, did it yell at you and tell you that you suck in bed? Do you have an abdominal scar from giving birth to it? Did the mechanic give it a $500 MRI and still find nothing wrong with it? Does it scream at you while you're trying to sleep? No? Shut up, then.

The two of you are like Starsky and Hutch, tearing down the street in your muscle car. (Okay, Jim and I are more like Klaus Kinski and Werner Herzog, holding each other at gunpoint and driving each other totally insane shooting *Aguirre, the Wrath of God*.) You will look at each other and know that you are the most asskicking pair of people that has ever existed. And some days you will have it so together that you are a four-armed, two-brained parenting machine, diapering and laundering and wiping and disciplining gently and arriving at playgroup perfectly on time. The two of you will barbecue in the backyard, supervising but not interfering during free play, while you crack a frosty beer and talk with the other breeders about psychotic exes and Internet porn. You will begin dressing alike. You may even get it on. You rock harder than Jon Spencer Blues Explosion.

Then there's the rest of the time.

"Are you aware that you treat Jim like a little boy?" The Good Therapist asked me once. "And that you always have to be right?"

"But I am right."

"Oh yeah? How's that working out for you?"

Not very well, I admitted.

Is it me? Him? Both of us? Sometimes it seems like everything we say to one another goes through a scrambling device that turns the most benign comments into stinging insults:

Jim says: "Would you mind endorsing these checks so I can make a deposit?"

I hear: "Would you pretty please get off your bonbon-eating, unemployed butt and sign these checks I've so laboriously assembled into a deposit while you were surfing the web, ignorant of our financial obligations?"

I say: "Why don't you go out this afternoon while Baldo and I stay here and play?"

Jim hears: "Since you're totally useless, why don't you leave the house and go jerk off at Best Buy for a while?"

But I just got a taste of my own medicine. Jim finally hit below the belt, talking out of pure frustration. He wanted to split up, and I was the one who should leave. I was making him miserable. Living with me was more stressful than he could handle. He hadn't been happy in two years. He was beginning to not care if I hurt myself after all. He was on his way to the post office in the car, and he'd been *this close* to just plowing into our neighbor's house.

And I finally listened. He was speaking my language! He was depressed! Jim, my man!

"Holy shit, it's got you, too!" I cried. It was so simple! We were *both* insane!

I knew Jim had some idiosyncrasies. He actively struggles with obsessive-compulsiveness. Early in our marriage, I awoke in the middle of the night to find his butt sticking out of the closet; he was furtively huddled over my shoe rack, organizing my footwear. If I brought groceries home and unloaded them in the kitchen, Jim would stand in the doorway, visibly twitching, until I moved out of his way and let him *reload them* in a manner that made sense to his brain. I follow your basic Betty Crocker guidelines: Put the vegetables in a drawer, put the raw meat on the bottom shelf so it won't drip on your cantaloupe and give you salmonella, right? Jim organizes them according to a template that exists only in his mind. For so long, I'd been trying to indulge these caprices without even realizing it.

His personality disorder hit the roof when we had a baby. Suddenly, there were all these new processes to obsess over. While he never explicitly said so, the cloth butt wipes had to be stacked in a special way: terrycloth side down, with the green printed ones on top and the white fluffy ones on the bottom. I just picked them out of the dryer and stuck them on top of the changer in a big pile. They were going to wipe baby ass! Who cares? I couldn't deal with these mysterious expectations and a screaming infant and wacky serotonin. There were antireflux medications to dispense and schedules to keep and sippy cups to clean. Pieces of things kept getting lost and outgrown. Socks fell off. Some sleepers zipped from the shoulder to the crotch, some of them buttoned down the front, some snapped up the back. Some of the towels were hooded, and some were plain. There was barf all over us and piles of laundry in the crib. We were steeped in chaos. Nothing was predictable. Our synapses sizzled like burning bacon. And fuck the shoes and groceries. No way was I going to even attempt to mimic Jim's organizational strategies. And who the fuck was he to expect me to?

I laid it all out for The Good Therapist in one of our sessions.

"Okay, give me all your judgments and assessments of Jim," she said, looking at her watch.

I vented my spleen. Jim is a slow talker, with lots of verbal pauses, those "uhs" and "umms," and he says "blah-blah" a lot when he can't think of a word, so much that now the baby is saying it, and he can't make a decision without involving me, whereas I just get about my business. He has to ask me about *everything*.

"Okay, stop. You find him irritating," she surmised. "You're smarter than he is, and you feel like he's pulling you down.

"But did you ever consider that that's how Jim demonstrates his love for you, by involving you in his choices? That it's a sign of respect? Appreciation?"

I hadn't. She had a point. It was time to reimagine where we were, where we had come from, where we were going. There was no other choice.

When Jim was apparently useless, when only I could bounce Baldo around the room in just the right way, when I wore the Baby-Björn all day and took naps in a chair, maybe there was admiration there. Maybe I never noticed because I was too busy tearing myself down. When my son clung to me and the tears fell for hours, no matter what I tried, maybe Baldo was acknowledging my strength. Maybe there was nothing in the world for him *but* me. Maybe when I was most dysfunctional, I was the only thing that worked.

Maybe, when Jim and I felt worlds apart, we were actually closer than ever.

LATEX

MY SON IS BORN INTO LATEX HANDS.

His grandmother puts a latex pacifier in his mouth.

His first toothbrush is a nubby latex thimble I put on my finger. I rub it along his gums, where buds of teeth like popcorn kernels have begun to emerge.

His first hairbrush is a rubber round brush. It is too small for me; when I use it to style myself, I look like an elderly woman with a recent wash-and-set, as in my wedding photos. But the baby loves it and will chew and chew on the handle while I change his diaper on the floor. I brush his sparse little butterscotch-colored hair and make a flip on the ends.

When we walk through the automatic doors at the natural-foods grocery store where I buy our esoteric, nonallergenic provisions, the smiling greeter hands him a latex balloon tied with a curly ribbon without me having to ask.

More latex balloons dot the floor of the coffeehouse where we attend free kids' concerts on Sundays. Gyrating toddlers toss them high, bounce them off the floor, abandon them to the eager hands of our baby. He licks them.

During our reflux phase, various healthcare providers poke and prod him with well-meaning fingers covered in latex.

Because I am too crazy to wash my own cloth diapers, and because there is so much vomit everywhere that the washing machine is already running constantly, we put the baby in disposable diapers with latex elastic.

When he has a cold, we irrigate the baby's nose with saline and suck out his mucus with a latex nasal bulb syringe.

We attend a kids' party with a "duckie" theme. Rubber duckies float in the wading pool, festoon the hallway, pop up in gift bags.

His eczema itches furiously, so we administer antihistamines daily with an oral syringe. The bulb is made of latex. The baby likes to chew on it and tantrums when we take it away.

He gets inoculations. Nurses apply pressure to the injection site with gauze pads and latex bandages.

He graduates to "big-boy shoes": sneakers with flexible rubber soles. He likes to trace the curlicues on the sole with his fingers.

We visit the home of Jim's teaching colleague, whose wife and new baby have just come home from the hospital. The child is an unbearably docile neonate. He cries only when I change his diaper. Then, mere steps of the baby shuffle lull him back into a contented slumber. Jim and I pass him back and forth, smelling his delicious head and exchanging meaningful glances. Approximately twelve oocytes ripen and burst from my ovaries, and I feel horny enough to meet every tour bus, eighteen-wheeler, and Army transport convoy breaching the Austin city limits on I-35. This is bad. We resolve to remain in neutral corners for the next forty-eight hours or until all my eggs are reabsorbed.

All the while, our toddler, who is by now almost nineteen months old, is making mischief with the new parents' barware, remote controls, and cordless telephone. Their lovely Crestview cottage is a maze of unprotected stairsteps, computer peripherals, bookcases, media towers, and knee-high antique bric-a-brac. Jim and I take turns hovering over Baldo, extracting risky items and distracting him with safe ones. He discovers a flashing, talking toy that sings the alphabet song.

"ABC!" he cries delightedly. He looks at me for confirmation. Our child is marvelous—so smart, really not very fussy anymore, exceptionally attractive. Wouldn't he love a little brother or sister? A tiny, sweet one? I creep back out in the hall to peep at Jim, who's cuddling the little ruddy pipsqueak and speaking sensitively to the new mother. What a great father he is. We've somehow survived being married to one another so far. Our fifth anniversary is next month. Shouldn't we have massive sex on top of the desk where Baldo was conceived?

I turn around to see that Baldo has located a cat toy and is busy exploring it with his mouth.

It's one of those ridiculous wands with a feather tied to a string. The opposite end has a rubber suction cup attached, so you can stick it to the wall for endless hours of feline self-amusement. This article is almost entirely inside my child's mouth.

This is bad for myriad reasons, such as the choking-hazard factor. The feline dander allergy factor. But we'll be hurtin' for certain the next day, when an angry red, raised rash covers my son's arms and legs in their entirety. I observe him scratching his knees in his sleep.

I've done enough research to know where latex is and where it isn't. I know which foods cross-react with it (avocados, bananas, and figs—all of which Baldo adores and craves). I know about the dangers of the hospital environment, about stethoscope tubing and CPR mannequins. I know about dangers in the home—about sock elastic and Koosh balls and swim goggles and bathing caps.

I mention my concerns to the pediatrician, and her response is to bang my son's knee with a rubber reflex hammer.

We return to the allergist for one last round of RAST testing. For the occasion, I wear my ass-kicking, knee-high platform boots. We listen to anger music in the car. The waiting room is full of grownups waiting for their weekly injections. I heft my son high and parade into the examining room for kids.

The walls are covered with juvenile artwork: renderings of the nurse who performs the pediatric skin-prick tests, pictures of rainbows and bunnies. "It doesn't hurt. Nope," writes one patient. It takes all the wind out of my sails, and I want to cry.

The doctor reminds me of a classics professor I had in college. It's been six months, so he goes over the baby's chart again. Wheat? Negative. Soy? Negative. Eggs? Slight positive. I tick off all the topicals we've tried on my fingers. The cat is gone. The eggs are gone.

Only 30 percent of children's eczema is caused by food sensitivities, he tells me. If the egg elimination didn't help, it's probably not the eggs.

"What is it?" I ask. "It has to be something, right? Can we find out?"

To me, this is the question any parent would ask. He answers with a shrug. "We'd be pulling stuff out of a hat," he admits, not dismissively but apologetically.

"I can't sit on my hands and wait for him to get better or worse," I say. "It's a quality-of-life issue."

"I understand your frustration." He probably does. I can't be the first person to harangue him like this.

We check the baby for signs of staph infection. None are present. I get debriefed again: *Keep the nails short. Use the antihistamine. Use the lotion five or six times a day if you have to.*

My lip's starting to go. I am not an ass-kicker. "It's just hard to do all this with a toddler." I feel like I'm whining. But it's just a statement of fact. Toddlers do not want to be lotioned six times a day. Mine bites me when I cut his nails, then bellows, "No bite!"

"Do you put gloves on him at night?"

I don't want to put gloves on him at night, and he doesn't want to wear them. I don't want to sneak into his room and try to put socks on his hands without waking him up. I don't want to do any of this shit. My son can undress himself by now. Yet he's not old enough to be reasoned with. Again, we will wait for this to pass. I am powerless against everything in my life. All I can do is wait for my life to pass.

The doctor agrees to test for latex. He is skeptical, of course, since my son is at no apparent risk for latex allergy. He has had no surgeries. He is not a healthcare worker. But surely I will be pacified when the result is negative.

The doctor then asks if there are other things I think he should test for, and I can't answer. *Everything?* I feel like an asshole.

So we go down to the lab on the building's first floor. A phlebotomist straps on latex examining gloves and ties my son's arm off with a latex tourniquet. When the draw is over she sticks a latex bandage over the puncture. I am too weak to protest. Besides, the bandage has Snoopy on it. "Doggie! Doggie!" Baldo giggles all the way home.

A week passes. The rash wanes. It flares up again after a snack of grapes and cantaloupe. I read about "Latex Fruit Syndrome," which involves not just bananas and avocados but potentially all "tropical" and "stone" fruits. Peaches. Plums. Nectarines. One article lists thirty-eight suspect fruits. Potatoes. Tomatoes. Another inculpates "cereals" and "peas." Still another suggests we avoid ragweed and grass pollens, papain (a enzyme derived from papaya and found in cosmetics, medications, and processed food), and the buttons on electronic equipment.

I am taking a shower when the allergist calls back.

"You're right," he says to the machine. "The test was positive for latex."

He is sending a packet of information by mail. None of the enclosures will tell me anything I didn't already know, but one is rather graphic in its depiction of secondary staph infection, eczema herpeticum, and lichenification of the popliteal fossa. A photograph displays an infant's horrible facial dermatitis ("Note the oozing and crusting skin lesions"). I am gladdened somewhat that it's not that bad, that we're being aggressive about treatment, that we're not being patted on the head and sent home with more Triamcinolone.

Our first task is to eliminate the latex from our environment. It's not unlike eliminating the nitrogen from the Earth's crust. I remove things one by one so as not to upset my son, who has become a typically mercurial toddler—wanting me to make the garbage truck come back and requesting cottage cheese for every meal. Out goes the adorable decorative throw rug in his bedroom, my one concession to juvenile cutesiness; it has a rubber non-slip backing, the kind kids' catalogs crow about to safety-minded guardians. Out goes our bath mat. Out go his teething toys, just in time for the canines to poke through. We buy latex-free diapers from the chichi, out-of-the-way grocery store, using them as backups to cloth. I solicit estimates for replacing our wall-to-wall carpeting with bamboo. Half of my office—my mouse pad, my rubber-grip pens, my headphones—will have to go. Our cute t-shirts with appliques. I read one note of warning about our vacuum cleaner's hose, which my son fondles and mouths with frenzied joy. We are fucked.

The new diet goes up on the wall. Its directives are precisely opposite to everything we've been told to eliminate previously. It's like living in an inverted world in which Superman is evil and Lex Luthor a superhero.

In	*Out*
SOYBEANS	BANANAS
DAIRY	AVOCADOS
MEAT, POULTRY, FISH	KIWIS
SQUASH	STRAWBERRIES
WHEAT	PAPAYA
EGGS	MANGO

Out cont.

WALNUTS
PLUMS
PEARS
APPLES
CARROTS
PEACHES
APRICOTS
GRAPES
NECTARINES
MELONS
POTATOES

Once more, my fury at Dr. Sears is rekindled: his elimination diet, with includes pears; his touting of papaya as "the perfect infant food"; his *Family Nutrition Book*, with its cover photo of three smiling, perfect, healthy Caucasian children noshing on forbidden watermelon, so rich in lycopene.

I'm starting to feel slaphappy, unable to read *Daddy and Me* with my customary vigor. So we retire to my office and play games on SesameStreet.com, games that inevitably involve the forbidden: banana peels in Oscar's trash collection, rubber balls that bounce, a "healthy breakfast" with peaches and kiwis. Everything that is wholesome and good in this world is bad for my son. Soon we'll outfit him with protective silicone goggles and enclose him in a Lucite bubble. We'll have to wrap him with aluminum foil and poke him with a fork so he doesn't explode.

At the playground, he pines for an older kid's tricycle, tries to scale it, raises a fuss. The kid is actually willing to share, but I still have to drag my son away, sit him down, hold his hands, talk him out of a tantrum. And again. Then once more. The handlebars are rubberized.

Jim and I take a deep breath and prepare to burst forth from the confines of our HMO and enter the world of alternative medicine. I am suspicious. He is pissed.

"I'm sick of putting all these lotions on my kid," he growls. "I'm sick of seeing him dig around in his diaper and bite his hands. Let's go for it."

I conduct an email exchange with a Michigan midwife who recommends the Nambudripad Allergy Elimination Technique, or NAET.

"It sounds like a crock," she admits. "But it works."

Truthfully, I am not a proponent of alternative medicine. I am a skeptic. I read Quackwatch. I distrust chiropractors. Yet neither am I a proponent of allopathic medicine. I also distrust gynecologists, internists, and podiatrists. (I do, however, love anesthesiologists and psychopharmacologists.) Just give me my Paxil and back off. Don't stick me with anything. Don't give me herbal tinctures. Don't tell me my energy is blocked, and that I need to meditate on my ninth chakra. Don't put me on steroids. Don't give me the birth control pill. It's a mindset I inherited from my forebears, hardy ranching types. We fall off our tractors, and our loyal working dogs pull us back to the house and treat us with Pabst and chili. I watched my father accumulate a subcutaneous mass in his arm the size of a ruby red grapefruit before he gave in and saw a doctor in town, who of course made an incision and evacuated the spot of twelve years' worth of sebum, then packed the socket with rolls upon rolls of gauze.

But that was before I had a kid who was allergic to everything. And there was precedent for complementary medicine: It had been practiced upon the family dog, Baggins. Baggins was a rickety basset who became more obstreperous and woeful with each of her fourteen years. She would snap at any hand that approached her. She would huddle on the carpet and whine; she would crimp up with pain in her joints, which were stressed by her considerable and weirdly distributed body mass. Yet Baggins, like the rest of the Howards, was no pantywaist. She'd once eaten an entire bag of Hershey's Kisses, including the foil. She'd scarfed up the contents of a knocked-over bottle of Advil. She'd been backed over by a truck. She was indestructible yet infirm.

When the country vet had exhausted his course of treatment for her, my parents sought the town acupuncturist, Dr. Lee. Dr. Lee was unaccustomed to work on dogs, so two small-animal doctors from the acclaimed veterinary school at nearby Texas A&M came to assist and witness the procedures, which were a cause célèbre throughout the county. After the treatments, Baggins was able to rise once more and shuffle to her food bowl (she was still a fourteen-year-old basset, after all).

So rather than apply topical steroids every day ("There aren't any side effects with a low dose," the allergist tells me with a straight face), we seek out a NAET practitioner in town. It turns out she's headquartered in a bank of office suites across the street from our favorite neighborhood bar, which is so packed at night that drinkers bring lawn chairs and camp in the parking lot. This is a good sign.

Meanwhile, we have stripped our house of its wall-to-wall

carpeting, leaving the rubber-backed plush menace intact only in our spare room and tiny office. We rip up the carpeting in Baldo's room, only to discover something worse underneath: asbestos tile. The living room and hallway are resurfaced with natural, vertical-cut bamboo, a process that takes just shy of a month between the first phone call and the final dot of caulk. Along the way, our materials will be quarantined in customs en route from China; our supplier will order the wrong finish; I will escape the house for a week with Baldo on my parents' farm, which I haven't seen since my flight to sanity six months ago. ("You could visit more often," my mom needles us.)

Yet the rash worsens to the point where Baldo wears his footed pajamas all day and night. He'll pull off any socks and shoes—even the vaunted leather Robeez—and scratch his feet bloody. I find faint pink streaks in his crib after naptime. We resume the steroid regimen, but by now even it doesn't seem to be helping. Even on Locoid, his face is mottled and welty, reminding me once more of *Eraserhead*: He looks like the Lady in the Radiator, sweetly juvenile but for his pustular cheeks. I am no longer annoyed by well-meaning strangers inquiring about his age or name. Now the first thing out of their mouths is, "Does he have a rash?"

I even feel fortunate to have found zip-front, toddler-sized, all-cotton footies in which to dress my kid. I harangued every children's store clerk in town to get them. *Not* polyester fleece—that breaks him out. *Not* button-front—he'll rip them open like The Incredible Hulk to scratch the discoid bumps on his belly. I don't *care* if they're made for boys or girls. I don't care if they're brown and have *butts* all over them. I strike pay dirt at A Certain National Children's Chain Store I usually avoid. Cotton, zippered toddler footies are in stock and on sale, and there's another mom with an eczema kid shopping in the store with me! We turn the racks inside out. "These are the only sleepers that work for us, too," she whispers conspiratorily. "I have four kids, and if the first three had been like him"—she crooks her thumb in the direction of her allergy kid, who's wheezing around the store—"there'd have been no more."

I feel maternally inadequate attiring my child in what are basically zippered jumpsuits, the kind people wear in futuristic movies from the 1960s. On the one hand, I am pleased to stop digging for socks in the dryer, to no longer match shirts and pants. We zip and go. I want my own jumpsuit. I find one pattern online, a vintage Pucci jumpsuit with flared palazzo legs. It's very Jackie Susann. I'll wear it with square sunglasses and go-go boots, and Baldo will be my funky little crime-fighting sidekick, Toddler Boy. On the other hand, children's clothes are so cute. The other children at the Sunday morning kids' concert look so adorable, especially in wintertime, with their knitted pompon caps and teeny cable-knit sweaters. They aren't wearing pumpkin jammies from the post-Halloween clearance rack. Sometimes I put a long-sleeved snapshirt over the jammies to disguise them. With his shirt snapped over his crotch and leggings underneath, Baldo looks like a fencer. All he needs are a helmet and an épée.

My heart and my Visa are heavy by the time we say goodbye to our shoe-molding installer and arrive at the office of the person we've begun to call, somewhat uncharitably, The Hoodoo Doctor.

She even has an eponymous theme song sung to the tune of Ween's "Voodoo Lady." This is unkind, but I am still skeptical.

My confidence is not inspired by the diagnostic procedure, which costs $150 and consists of touching Baldo with a Very Beepy Peripheral Device attached to a laptop computer. He's so squirmy that the doctor tells me to touch the Very Beepy Peripheral Device while making skin-to-skin contact with Baldo. "You're the conduit," she explains. My bullshit detector hits Defcon 1. Just the same, we are unable to get through more than half of the potential allergens we can test for before Baldo wriggles free from my grasp and scurries into the treatment room, where he turns off the ambient New Age music and uproots a small ponytail plant. I try to replace the plant in its pot, but it still leans at a crazy angle. I decide not to mention it.

The device sings a cantata of beeps for the following substances: cat dander, eggs, and peanuts, which we already knew about. Also indicated were two new suspects: caffeine and corn.

"Does he eat or drink caffeine?" the doctor asks.

My face reddens. I have been eating a lot of dark chocolate. I also had corn enchiladas the night before, and we start every day with bowls of Kix (first ingredient: cornmeal).

Because we don't finish the tests, the doctor offers to perform the first treatment in the course of therapy instead, for the same price. This seems reasonable. Hell, it all seems reasonable at this point, now that I am hemorrhaging money on $19 sleepers and hardwood flooring.

Scarcely an hour after the first treatment, I can't recall the explanations given by The Hoodoo Doctor as she handed me a glass jar containing a vial of an unknown substance and applied what appeared to be a small battery-operated vibrator to various pressure points on my body while Baldo squirmed shirtlessly on my stomach. There was something about energy moving. Then she instructed us to sit in a chair quietly for fifteen minutes, maintaining contact with each other and the jar. I felt like an asshole, nursing my child on one arm and holding a jar of God-knows-what with the other. But I did feel *strangely warm*. Baldo, who had been twisting and whining and uprooting plants, sagged against my stomach and fell asleep.

We made another appointment for the following Monday.

The first treatment was for "brain and body function," which balances one's humours, or something. Then we proceeded through a series of twelve treatments intended to allow Baldo's inflamed body to process nutrients properly.

Jim reads through the pamphlet from the doctor. "This is total horseshit," he observes.

"But wait," I pipe. "I'm the conduit. That's the best part."

I am unprepared for the calcium treatment, which would necessitate the cessation of nursing for a twenty-five-hour period.

"Well, the treatments are in that order for a reason," the doctor sniffs. "But we'll ask his body if we can skip ahead to sugar." She holds her fist to her head and concentrates for a moment, like the Amazing Kreskin, then lays her hand on my arm.

"His body says we can do sugar today," she concludes. And so we avoid all forms of sugar, including the pernicious corn syrup, for the next twenty-five hours. Deprived of yogurt and string cheese,

Baldo tantrums furiously and clings to me like moss. When the twenty-fifth hour concludes, we charge the kitchen and load up on Goldfish crackers.

"I've got to see this," Jim insists. He accompanies us to the session on vitamin C the day before Thanksgiving, but the doctor boots him from the treatment room.

"Your energy is disruptive. You might end up receiving the treatment instead of Baldo," she proclaims. We look at each other. He shrugs and retreats to the waiting room.

That afternoon his parents arrive from California. His mother is a retired critical care nurse, and his father a retired litigator for an insurance corporation. I despair of how to explain our treatment regimen. Surely we look like sage stick–smudging, chicken-decapitating weirdies. As it happens, I am able to disguise the vitamin C fast in the form of the Typical American Diet—hamburgers and chicken strips—until our twenty-five hours elapse and we dig into Thanksgiving dinner.

Jim's mother hangs in the doorway with her nebulizer, coughing wetly and tearily. "It's my allergies," she says, waving her hand dismissively. I had mated with this woman's offspring, unaware of her asthma, her hay fever, and her myriad allergies. Cats. Pollen. Shellfish. And latex.

"Oh, my, yes." She pauses to huff albuterol. "He gets that from me. At the hospital they had to order special cotton inserts for me to put inside my gloves so my skin wouldn't break out. And when they put my stent in, that physician *insisted* I be given Betadine, although I *told* that nurse I was allergic to iodine and I *arrested* on the table."

Jim shows her the rash on Baldo's back. His skin feels like sandpaper all over. And something in her manner toward us changes.

"That's more than food," she declares. We all scratch our heads, then retreat to the backyard for a rousing game of Nut Ball, so named for the object of play—a pecan that is rolled with sticks into a trash can on our back porch. Baldo loves the game so much that I say "Nut Ball" without a trace of self-consciousness. When I mention it to men, they instinctively shrivel and make a fig leaf with their hands.

Upon returning from the yard, Baldo is noticeably rashier. We recount the contents of Thanksgiving dinner: Asparagus, turkey, cornbread stuffing, a bite of pumpkin pie for Baldo, and a slice of pecan for me. Water. Jell-O. Corn syrup in the pie? We've been cleared for eggs. Could it be eggs?

That night Baldo awakens three or four times, screaming, itching, inconsolable. Jim applies lotions. I curl up on my pillow and cry; I'm forbidden to help. I can't go back to sleep, even after the wailing has subsided. Even though I remind myself that this would have been a typical night for us one year ago, due to the reflux, and is now horrible and anomalous. Is that progress?

I get up for good at 5:45 to resume the rocking and cuddling. By now Baldo asks for it specifically. "Hold you," he whispers, collapses onto me. Jim slinks off to catch some sleep before the gauntlet of post-Thanksgiving family activities ensues, but twenty minutes later he materializes, wild eyed, beside me as I'm gazing into the luminous, galactic swirl of soy milk inside my herbal coffee-like beverage and Baldo conforms to my leg.

"Nuts!" he cries, like Tony McAuliffe fighting the Battle of the Bulge.

"Huh?"

"It's those fucking pecans."

Of course! How could it not have been obvious? I slap my forehead. Then again, it's not as if any of our various advisers suggested it to us. *Do you have massive skin contact with tree nuts, perhaps in the form of a whimsical game your child enjoys greatly?*

One of the signs of prosaic suburban adulthood is that you have your own arborist. We, in fact, do—he's an earthy fellow with Maori tattoos and a dude-like mien. He is also a childhood eczema sufferer, having been plagued with rashes and carbuncles until the age of thirteen. His continued presence upon the earth is a comfort to me; I imagine Baldo grown up and dude-like, swinging from the very trees that sickened him in his youth. I imagine him operating a chain saw and a chipper. I imagine him loaded on peyote and wandering around Big Bend, which is what the tree crew does during their staff retreat.

Needless to say, the arborist is distressed by the prospect of extracting our two gorgeous and fully mature hybrid pecans, which disgorge a tasty and bountiful harvest every other year. I dream of baking pecans into pies, candying them, crushing them over sautéed *haricots verts.* My own crop. A deep and very real source of pride for the Texan settler. Food that grows on my land. I'd cherished my pecans. I'd refused weed-and-feed or anything that might taint the drip line. I tied my clothesline around them. I'd spread a Mexican blanket in their shade during the peak of my insanity, weeping with the baby on my lap until at last I felt sheltered, embraced, reassured that in their years the trees had seen tearful mothers come and go, had seen every kind of human pain, had seen love die, had seen despair triumph over the spirit, and yet had lived. They would, however, not survive my son's medical peccadilloes.

"Maybe we could, like, catch the nuts in a *net*," the arborist suggested.

"Do you have such a net?" Jim asked.

"No."

What of the pollen, the gauzy blobs of bagworm chrysalis that drop from the branches, which my son loved to impale upon a stick and fling through the air in a sort of toddler jai alai? Where were the allergens concentrated? I imagined the molecules, spiky and bulbous, making my child cry.

I hang my hopes once more upon The Hoodoo Doctor, who writes "pecans" in her notebook and instructs us to avoid iron for twenty-five hours. "We can clear that. And the peanuts, probably in one more treatment."

We shop for iron-free foods on the way home: a bag of frozen chicken and a big head of cauliflower. We are also planning a party on the weekend, so I decide to stock up on beer in advance of buying the perishables. I load the cart with three six-packs and a giant bottle of assy Texas wine. "Beer! Beer!" Baldo cries. Other shoppers look askance at me, my cart full of cauliflower and beer. No apples, no cheese, none of the wholesome foods depicted in Baldo's picture books. No raisins, no juice, no sandwich makings. No crackers with sesame seeds.

"But I'm a good mother," I whimper to myself. "I'll try anything."

We prepare for the daunting treatment for minerals. Baldo must abstain from touching metal for twenty-five hours. I'm not even sure how we're supposed to get home without touching metal—the doorknob, the car keys, the latch on his toddler seat.

"Don't you have gloves?" The Hoodoo Doctor asks.

I sneer. Has she talked to the allergist? There are no cotton gloves in toddler sizes. Toddler gloves are puffy and made of Polarfleece for cold climates. They are tied together so they won't get lost. They are not well suited to indoor wear. The doctor gives me some plain cotton gloves from her drawer, the smallest available juvenile size, but still giant on my son: The fingers droop and Baldo laughs. Twenty-five hours?

I can't pin the gloves to his sleeves because of the metal, so I get crafty and decide to sew them on to a plain cotton pullover with plastic buttons and no snaps at the bottom. It's a *gloveshirt*. So I sit on the couch one evening with my sewing basket, pincushion strapped to my wrist. I line one of the too-long gloves up with the shirt's elastic cuff (I hope they don't have latex in them) and stitch around in a circle.

"Voilà!" I flourish the gloveshirt, half-finished.

Jim cocks his head, perplexed.

"Goddammit." I have sewn the glove on backwards. The thumb is where the pinky should be. I am not skilled.

Even The Hoodoo Doctor laughs at my handiwork. The fingers dangle from Baldo's sleeves like flayed flesh.

Because I do not plan to stop nursing during the mineral fast, I too must refrain from exposure. I make a cup of black Postum with distilled water in a ceramic mug, stirring with a plastic spoon. The lid of the Postum is metal. The handle to the cupboard is metal.

I steam cauliflower in distilled water. When this is over, I am never eating cauliflower again.

For meals I remove the gloveshirt, leaving Baldo in a pair of cotton sweatpants with socks sewn to the cuffs and leather slippers on top. Thus attired, he looks like Bruce Lee in *Enter the Dragon*, aside from the obvious ethnic differences: small, wiry, scrappy, scratched across his chest, ready for a street fight with unfriendly protein chains. Instead I give him Jell-O and cauliflower. Dinner is unfortified white rice cooked in a crockpot with unseasoned ground beef.

"Meat mush!" I cry, brandishing my wooden spoon. "Yum!"

Wearing the gloveshirt, he tries to turn the pages of board books and stack blocks, then gives up and cries to play in the backyard. I open the sliding glass door with my elbows, and he immediately runs to our chain-link perimeter fence and *licks* it. I sag down to the ground and lie there, surrounded by pecans.

"You licked the fence!"

Baldo giggles.

Next we eliminate salt. I am careful to banish from the kitchen any item with sodium. Even broccoli is too salty. I shop for two more jugs of distilled water and squash. We can't have frozen blueberries—the only fruit my kid can tolerate—so I get a package of fresh ones, shipped from Argentina. It's December. They cost $5.99.

A produce stocker stops us. "That rash looks awful," he says.

Naturally, I've got my back up. I start to respond.

"My grandbaby has fifth disease. Just scratches all the time. It's so hard on a family."

I start to cry.

We have also become suspicious of the lotion we apply. It has lanolin. Jim confirms that his mother, who evidently has no immune system whatsoever, is also sensitive to lanolin. I root through the lotions on the shelf. *Lanolin. Lanolin alcohol. Lanolin.* Lanolin is gentle enough for little lambs. Postpartum mothers put pure medical-grade lanolin on their nipples. Lanolin is like sunshine and the laughter of children.

I find a lotion without it. It seems plain enough—just cetyl alcohol and petrolatum. The methylparaben preservative may be a problem, but we'll have to risk it.

What I don't realize at the time is that the lotion is full of sodium preservatives. In other words, the forbidden salt.

Baldo wants to play with Play-Doh. I pull our bag of it out of the cabinet. We are pressing shapes into it, naming them. *That's a trapezoid.* I breathe and smile. It's kinesthetic learning. I'm rooting around in my brain for the definition of a scalene triangle, obtained all those years ago from my geometry teacher, Mr. Sprunk, when I realize the Play-Doh is also full of salt.

"Oh, fuck this!" I zip up the bag and put it away.

On the other hand, the corn elimination is barely even noticeable because we don't eat corn anyway. I can't drink my usual Postum because it contains maltodextrin derived from corn. But that's it.

After New Year's, a rotavirus strikes the house. Baldo vomits for four days. We are blasé.

"Do you remember," I ask Jim, "when every day was like this?"

Baldo pukes into our cupped hands. I try to teach him to void over the side of the bathtub, but he pulls away and collapses into my arms again. He wants to vomit *on me*.

When he becomes visibly dehydrated from the rotavirus, we visit Urgent Care.

"And what do we have here?" the nurse asks. "Looks like a big, raised rash." She starts scribbling in her notebook.

"No, it's a rotavirus," we correct her. "We're not here for the rash."

The next two doctors we see make the same mistake. When Baldo is admitted to the ER and given a gown to wear, we have to hold his arms at his sides to keep him from scratching.

By now he asks to be put in his jammies. *Wear jammies. Close up sleeves. Get pins.*

The mother of a boy with a broken arm points to Baldo's broken skin. "I have to ask: Is that a vaccine reaction?"

"No, he's always like this."

Cedar season strikes, and Baldo begins raining snot. Austin is the allergy capital of the world, no kidding. The Hoodoo Doctor does some kind of hand jive on him while Baldo is running past her to activate the spigot on her water cooler. "He's reacting to cedar. Everyone is."

Next up is rice. Rice, the benign grain. Baby's first solid food. I ate bowls and bowls of rice on the Dr. Sears elimination diet. Rice pasta. Rice flour in Baldo's first birthday cake. Rice milk. Rice crackers. When we were desperate to keep Little Baldo from throwing up all his breast milk during the reflux phase, doctors advised us to thicken it with rice in a bottle. When Little Baldo couldn't sleep for more than forty-five minutes at a stretch, my mother arrived in the driveway, brandishing a box of rice cereal. Insisting.

"I gave it to you in your bottle when you were three weeks old," she said. "You slept right through the night." We wanted to resist, but we couldn't. We were tired. We needed help.

The allergist all but refused to perform a RAST for rice. It's the least allergenic food substance there is, he said, when I asked him. But we know people can be allergic to it. Jim has a highly allergic child in one of his eighth-grade English classes. He's allergic to rice.

I remember months ago, when Baldo's eczema had just cropped up and the pediatrician was sweating us to wean him, how we'd happened upon a "special report" about food allergies on our local news. It contained the story of a two-year-old girl—adorable, playful, totally allergic to everything, rice included. She had a team of doctors—managing her skin care, managing her breathing.

Our suspicions seem to be confirmed when Jim slips Baldo a rice cake while grocery shopping. By the time they get home, Baldo's hands are raw from scratching. He's screaming.

"I just forgot," Jim admits. "I can't remember what he's allergic to and what he isn't."

So when the time comes, we lie atop the table in The Hoodoo Doctor's examining room. Baldo squirms shirtlessly on my belly. I hold the jar full of the rice essence in one hand and The Hoodoo

Doctor performs the muscle test for allergy on my other arm. I still don't totally hold with this stuff, the applied kinetics and acupressure. And maybe it's the power of suggestion, but when The Hoodoo Doctor pushes down on my arm and orders me to resist, I'm as weak as a kitten. The Hoodoo Doctor is a grandmotherly lady. It galls me that she can push me around. Me, the stocky, pie-eating Swede. She pushes me around like I'm her jailhouse bitch.

"Can we try that again?" I ask. We do.

"That's a strong reaction to rice," she notes.

"Did you cut your hair?" I ask. "It looks nice."

She beams. "Thanks." We see each other twice a week now, so why not notice these things?

Should I go back and insist on a RAST? Do I need allopathic medical confirmation? Will I have to go and drop $75 for a visit and however much on lab fees every time? Am I going to be wearing hemp skirts and shopping at the co-op forever? I feel squirrely at the co-op, as if everyone there knows I don't belong. They know I'd just as soon swing by Albertson's, break the grocery strike, and grab a box of Zingers to eat in the car. I secretly *want* guar gum. I feel like a fink when I park my big hunk of European steel in the parking lot, when I use my evil credit card to pay. (Then again, I guess they don't have to accept it, do they?) Will ours be a life without food additives? A box of organic macaroni and cheese costs $1.29. I'm going to have to get a real job, or else Jim is. I'm going to have to get into advertising. I'm going to have to work at a corporation so I can afford to shop independent. What kind of irony is that? I'm going to be the weird hippie mother who slaps jelly beans out of her kid's hand at the roller rink. We're going to have to find jellybeans sweetened with cane juice. They'll all be brown. They're going to cost $5 apiece and taste like carob.

Unless this Hoodoo thing works.

A friend of mine practices actual Voudou. "You know," she suggests gingerly, "you could do the real thing." I'm just not sure about that yet. She's come into town for the Lave Tet ceremony with her Mambo. Later she will tell me that after her ritual cleansing, she coughed up a strange wrinkled mass of pink, wet tissue the size of a golf ball.

But then something *really* weird starts to happen: Baldo's skin starts to clear up. We continue the NAET treatment, testing for and clearing sensitivities to nuts and latex and dander. Then I discover a half-used tube of Protopic ointment from the dermatologist and apply it to the boy, on a whim. It didn't work before, but the next morning Baldo's skin is appreciably less inflamed.

First to go are the welts on his back. Then the welts on his tummy. His face clears up, then his butt rash. His feet are still dry and blotchy. His hands are still itchy, but his face is as pale and smooth as a just-opened tub of margarine. His skin doesn't feel thin. His cheeks feel plumper. I touch them frequently. It's nice.

Periodically, something will inflame him moments after he eats it. These items we record on a sheet of scratch paper. Artificial sweeteners? Broccoli? Gelatin? I dimly recall that there is a substance in the skins of hard fruits that is chemically similar to gelatin. Pectin? My mother used it when making preserves. After Baldo eats some Jell-O at Luby's—a birthday tradition in my family—he gets red and itchy through the face. Squirms in his seat. Fusses to get up. I squirm too. Already I have proven myself a crap mother by forgetting my diaper bag in the garage at home. Since I don't have my license, my mom has to drive. I am humiliated by my child's discomfort.

My mother snorts. "It's not important, dear."

"No, it is," I insist. I'm supposed to figure these things out, right? I'm supposed to note every reaction and determine its source and feed my child a wholesome, healthful diet, right?

"I'm almost ready to go, anyway," my dad insists.

"No, let's stay and finish our lunch." Now my child has begun throwing macaroni and wailing. Now is when I'm supposed to bust out the discipline. Not too gentle; not too strict. I am supposed to socialize him to sit down throughout a meal and respect the appetites of others, their desire to converse. "Want out! Want out!" he yells.

"Let's get your pie to go," my mom suggests.

"Pectin," I write on the list. "Olive oil. Citrus. Mushrooms. Broccoli (hand biting). Pears. Herbs? Echinacea. Tomatoes (too acidic?). Food dyes. Pectin."

"This is insane," I tell Jim. "I'm afraid to eat or serve anything."

We go to a baby shower at a municipal park with a wading pool. One of the other dads watches Jim struggling with Baldo to keep him from scratching his feet.

"Oh, hey," the dad says. "He has eczema, right?"

"So you can tell."

The guy laughs. "Man, I had it so bad when I was a kid. I had to go to the hospital, and they tied down my hands so I wouldn't scratch. It was pretty gnarly."

This sounds horrible to me, but the other dad is blasé and practically cheerful about it.

"And then I guess I grew out of it."

When we end up at the ER after an accidental exposure to sesame seeds hidden in some meatballs, the two of us make an executive decision: We will focus on the exclusion of life-threatening allergens, instead of chasing the chimera of food sensitivities. We know peanuts and tree nuts are bad. We have gathered from our meatball follies that sesame seeds are likewise. We will continue to exclude shellfish in the event that Baldo has inherited his grandmother's shrimp thing. And that's it. Not that I'm planning to pump him full of red dye #40, but I'm not going to drive myself back to the brink of insanity, either.

Back come the avocados. The bananas. I stuff the kid with wheat and soy. I also start stuffing him with flaxseeds. We keep a Rolodex of dermatologists for our Protopic prescriptions.

And it really does get better slowly. Just the way everything else seems to.

A TANTRUM

THE BABY IS NOW THE TODDLER. It really is getting easier.

Everyone said it would. *This too shall pass*, they said. *The way out is through*, they said. Kindly platitudes to mollify me, but they were true. Now I believe mothers when they say the things that mothers say.

I still have days when anxiety sickens me, when I want to punch people out. And when I say "I want to punch people out," I am to be believed. This is not an idle, hypothetical threat; this is an actual clenched fist, holding in my anger. Their stupid remarks reverberate when I am falling asleep at night, and I inevitably ask myself what I haven't done, what I haven't tried to be a better mother, to be a better person.

A trip to the farmers market leads to a conversation with a homeschooling mother of seven, a flower-grower whose offspring are assembling bunches of blossoms and greenery for Clarksville yuppies. One of her children attended Jim's class after he was mainstreamed into the public school system, and the two of them are catching up next to a bucket of sunflowers. Which leaves me to chat up the mother—about her flowers, about her kid, about my kid.

"Are you still at home with him?" she asks.

"Yes," I say, "and I'm finishing my first book."

"Isn't it great? I just love being at home with mine."

I could point out that neither she nor her family is actually at home, but downtown in the midst of activity. Instead I just smile and nod.

"Really, I hear women complain about being home with their kids, and I just want to slap them! We had so much fun, didn't we, sweetie?" Jim's former student, who's just been on his first trip to Europe and is the valedictorian of his current school and is by all accounts a perfect citizen, waves his agreement. "We had a loom, and I'd weave, and we just all had a great time," she continues.

I'm still formulating answers to this. *It's not being home I complain about. It's about being isolated and forgotten and left to handle all this by myself, about having doctors who push formula, steroids, nebulizers and pat me on the head and send me home again. It's about insanity. It's about me sticking your loom up your precious ass.*

But really I just want to hurt myself as quickly as I can, using whatever's handy—a wall to hit, teeth to bite, fingernails to dig. I have no words for my anger. I only know how to turn it into pain.

Apparently, the same is true for toddlers.

I had a setback when Baldo threw his first bona fide shitfit. I denied him something inconsequential; I can't even remember what it was—maybe I told him it was time to change his crapped-in diaper. No crying, no yelling—he just smashed his forehead right into the wall. Flopped down, beat himself against the floor. Reached out and took my hand and bit it.

It's scary to watch a little kid rage. If you're trying to get over hurting yourself, it's a bigger deal. All you can do is hold him still, put your hand between his forehead and the floor, try to get his arms at his sides and your fingers out of his mouth, tell him, "I know you're angry. Be angry, but I'm not going to let you hurt yourself, because I love you." And as you're saying it, you know you've heard it before and it didn't make a difference to you. Why should it make a difference to him?

All you can do is put faith in ratiocination. Hope that your kid realizes that he can put a word to a feeling and scream it out loud. An act of cognition is taking place. He'll recognize his anger, articulate it, describe it, examine it, survive it. And so will you.

I infuriate my child. I take hazards out of his hands—a package of batteries I hadn't realized was open, the Boudreaux's Butt Paste he wants to squirt directly into his mouth. I close the refrigerator door when he wants it open. He wants to scratch the dermatitis on his feet, and I want to cram him into his cotton footies. I sit him down to lotion him. I insist that we go back inside when the mosquitoes are biting. I hear other mothers in my mind, better mothers: *I created an environment in our home that says yes!* The fuck you did. Your kid wants to run out into the street, just as mine does.

It helps that I must categorically deny my child certain pleasures in life. He'll never have those weird orange peanut-butter crackers you get in truck-stop vending machines. He can't eat Halloween candy or his friend Lily's sesame sticks. We can't follow the "natural consequences" method. And here my background as a crazy person, as an addict and a friend of addicts, comes in handy. Maybe it doesn't help for me to hold him so tightly, to cry with him, to tell him everyone gets frustrated and angry and wants what they can't have, but at least I know how to do so.

As time went by, the universe threw me a bone. My child grew into a deliciously verbal toddler. He talks as urgently as he used to bash and bite. His feelings are extreme, like mine. He falls apart when he's frightened—by big trucks, sharks, by scarecrows, by loud kids on the playground. He catches an episode of *Teletubbies* at a friend's house and sobs hysterically when Noo-noo the vacuum cleans up a splatter of Tubby custard, or whatever that shit is. "No TV!" he screams. "We will not watch TV!" His two toddler friends look at him blankly. For weeks afterward, he talks about the incident. I tell naptime stories about it upon request. *And then Valerie turned off the television and made the noisy machine go away.* He smiles.

We might as well go ahead and write him out a scrip for Paxil.

The world is not kind to my son. I fear he'll be small and sensitive and an easy target for bashers. He's going to feel things deeply. He'll probably wear black and discover The Smiths. (For about a week, he asked to hear a song he called "This Way and That Way," which I could only assume was the morose ballad "Stretch Out and Wait." He'd actually meant the kiddie classic "Have You Ever Seen a Lassie?" which I guess he heard someplace happier.)

On one of my first evenings without the baby, I went to a friend's house party. One of the other women was reading palms, a practice I regard incredulously, skeptic that I am.

"You were tormented with thumbscrews in a previous lifetime for being too educated," she concluded. "And look over here," she added. "There's your son. You'll have one child. He chose you."

He chose you. Reverse causation was a ridiculous notion, even when Schopenhauer advanced it. But it feels that way sometimes. My baby made me his bitch. He stretched me to the limit of my compassion. He broke my spirit and made me rebuild it so I would be strong enough to love him.

With equal passion he extols what he loves—including me.

"Marrit," he says, for that's what he calls me.

"Yes?"

"I love ya."

He says it so quickly, so offhandedly. Yet we have this exchange in the car, in the bathtub, at the dinner table, while we're playing with stamps or markers or Play-Doh. And in these moments, I discover that I am healed. We are healing ourselves together. We are fierce and strong in love. Sometimes he is a little fart, but I know I will never be closer to another person.

POSITIVE THOUGHTS

IN SPITE OF EVERYTHING, I have fallen in love with my child.

When he nurses, he runs his fingers along my other arm and threads them through mine. His hand feels spidery.

I tell him, "Nose to nose," and he leans into my face and presses his nose to mine. We sit like that for several seconds.

He laughs for the first time in the doctor's office. He is six months old. I have him propped up in my lap in the waiting room; Jim sits next to us. A dad at the counter is fumbling with some paperwork and a stapler. He drops the stapler, and it goes *sproing!* onto the floor. Baldo guffaws. "Oh, you think that's funny, do you?" the guy asks, not altogether kindly. Baldo laughs harder. We hadn't realized that he knew how to laugh.

At thirteen months, he finds his penis. (He's a late bloomer.) We say, "Where's your penis?" and he points to it and smiles cheesily. I say, "And where's your shoulder?" Again, he points to his penis.

He loves broccoli.

He has just started walking. When I finish giving him a bath one morning, he holds my hand, and we walk back to his room together to put clothes on. It's like walking hand in hand with a tiny naked alien. Our silhouettes on the wall make me laugh.

I like the way his nose breaks out in a sweat when he's falling asleep.

At sixteen months, he falls in love for the first time, with a wait-ress named Amy. "Amy, Amy!" he yells whenever we eat in a restaurant. I point to our alphabet blocks: B-U-S. "What does that say?" "Amy!"

Now he is nineteen months old, and he says things that amuse me:

"Hey, man!" he shouts, at no one. We recognize this as the refrain from David Bowie's "Suffragette City." "Bye-bye, baby balls," he calls as I fasten his diaper. Soundgarden comes on the radio. I tell him about how punk broke. "Grunge!" he yells.

One day he says, without prompting, "I'm happy."

He is fascinated with *bulgogi*, or Korean barbecue. We have to omit the sesame seeds because of his allergies.

"What should we have for breakfast?" *"Bulgogi!"*

"What color is that?" *"Bulgogi!"*

"Did you sleep well?" *"Bulgogi!"*

I draw a dog with floppy ears and wooly blue fur.

"What should her name be?" I ask.

"Bulgogi!"

He likes to point to my tattoo, under my collarbone.

"Spot," I say.

He points to my piercing.

"Dot," I say.

He begins to sing. It makes a difference.

Now that he is almost two, I can inject some of my personality into my parenting. I continue to mop up spills almost constantly, but I begin to feel more like myself.

He likes jokes. One long-running favorite is a joke about our dermatologist, Dr. Kaiser.

"What if Dr. Kaiser were a monster?" I ask, and I yell, *"Raaaaaah-hhhhrr!"* while checking an imaginary medical chart.

"What if Dr. Kaiser were Yoko Ono?" I ask and ululate passionately.

Sometimes Dr. Kaiser is underwater. Sometimes he is a chicken. Sometimes he is eating a mouthful of apples.

I teach the boy songs: "Pepino the Italian Mouse," "Bamboo House," "Ocean Man." While I am cooking cream of wheat, I sing "Kinky Boots," mugging and pantomiming in my pajamas. It is worth noting that I am on a rather high dose of Paxil. Surely it's cool to have a mom who sings like Honor Blackman instead of bleating out endless verses of "The Wheels on the Bus," but Baldo is not impressed. "Bye-bye," he says, waving to my mouth. "No sing."

I'm not bothered when he refuses to hug me, when he asks me to be quiet. *He's a person! He has desires and preferences!* I'm so used to thinking of him as subhuman.

We have a party for the holidays. He meets a new friend, a fourteen-month-old girl. He walks right over to her and hugs her gently. She stands there, impassive. Neither one's expression changes.

Now that he is almost two, I can have conversations with other parents about our children. I don't want to push these parents in front of oncoming traffic the way I used to. They'd beam and say, "Isn't it wonderful?" when their kids took their first steps, when they ate avocado, when they laughed at the cat. Their children were perfect and delightful. Mine was small and sick and fussy and had unexplained rashes.

Now their children are older, their personalities emergent, their bodies complicated. The parents tell me stories that resonate: a sweat test for cystic fibrosis, concerns about seizure disorders and late talking, a stubborn fever, biting and tantrums. Schadenfreude is not what I feel; I feel camaraderie at last. *This* is parenthood. Our children do not exist to please us. They exist for themselves, and we hurry to smooth their path. Just as in love and family relationships, we are our strongest selves when we are challenged. At last I recognize these people around me. They have metamorphosed from picture-taking chuckleheads to fellow journeymen. It is good for all of us to have each other.

It is good for all of us to have each other.

Now he is two and a half. Again he finds my tattoo. "You have a tattoo," he says.

"I do," I tell him. "And I want to get another one."

"Let's go tomorrow," he says. And we go to the tattoo shop, where I get a picture from his favorite bedtime book inked on the arm I use to hold him.

At lunchtime I struggle to open a package of cheese with a resealable zipper closure. My fingernails are too short. "Dammit," I mutter. "I can't open this cheese."

"You can do it, Marrit," he tells me solemnly.

You can do it, Marrit.

He wants to get a cat and name it Burl.

I pretend I am a mother gorilla. I grab him under my arm and lumber across the living room. His laughter is like prayer chimes. "Again!" he says. "You are a gorilla."

We find a drum kit, minus the stool, at the thrift store and buy it. It sits in the garage until we can make room for it inside. Whenever we go out to my car, he has to stop and play the drums.

"Do the big rock 'n' roll finish, and then let's get in the bus." The bus is my wagon, the car I wanted to die in.

He crashes the cymbal. "Goodnight, ladies and gentlemen," he says. Then he does a thing where he raises both arms high. "I am tipping the waitstaff."

Four months shy of his third birthday, I make my first trip away from home since the hepatitis episode. I fly to Toronto for a conference so I can flog this book to rooms full of feminist academics whose research deals with the political and cultural contexts of mothering. I stay in a giant generic hotel, and as I lie in my bed at night with the tang of homesickness practically in my mouth, I send Baldo dreams across time and space. I send him dreams of flowing water and diffuse sunlight, dreams of being held and loved. I send him slow and steady breaths; I send him the stillness around me.

I will send him dreams for the rest of my life.

THE UNITED STATES
OF GENERICA

I WANT PICTURE PEOPLE TO BURN, motherfucker, burn.

Our story begins with Julie, our photographer, who probably got this job by talking about how she just *loves* kids. I bet she has a niece or a nephew. She's probably very nice.

But if she doesn't get that rainbow-colored feather duster out of my kid's face, I'm going to wrestle her to the floor and shove it up her ass.

Each time she waggles the duster in Baldo's face she makes a great, ululating cry, like Xena: Warrior Princess. I can't imagine anyone being amused by this. Perhaps some children are sufficiently chuckleheaded to smile at her capering, her loathsome propeller beanie, her safari vest with epaulets, but mine is not. Mine has dissolved into a weeping mass on the floor of the storefront photography studio.

There are rooms in back that are quieter, that are full of toys for children to actually handle and enjoy, but Corporate Policy dictates that we will occupy the first room—the one in view of the foot traffic in the mall. Presumably, the sight of my child posing with props will melt casual pedestrians into gooey submission, their wallets oozing $10 sitting fees for their own grandkids and offspring.

If Julie stands him in front of the blue background holding an over-sized Valentine's heart—which she actually suggests—customers will stream to the service desk and join the Photo Club.

I resent this on principle—my son is not a posable Precious Moments action figure built to advertise their services, and if he'd rather stand on the stool than sit on it, why can't Julie just pho-tograph that?—but also because Baldo is clearly nonplussed by the pressure. He doesn't understand why he can't climb into the giant, multicolored, camera-shaped playhouse that is paces away; he doesn't understand why Julie keeps crossing his feet. Nor do I.

"Can't we just leave his feet uncrossed?" I wonder, after he sags into a natural bowlegged repose one more time.

"I don't want to get the bottom of his feet." Julie is readjusting her lens.

"Hold you," Baldo sobs, collapsing into my arms.

"Let's stand on this blue paper and look at Julie's camera," I suggest cheerily. I extend my arms, but Baldo is still wadded up into a tiny ball, his feet tucked, tears squeezing from his eyes. I set him down on the paper.

He stays in place but isn't smiling, so Julie ululates and tick-les him with the feather duster. Has this woman any knowledge of the toddler psyche? I worry that we appear stupid to the other par-ents looking on. There are two three-year-old twins with luxuriant, brown, bow-topped hair and matching pink sweater sets looking on as if the scenario is routine and Baldo's behavior is afoul of it. Ours is a topsy-turvy world if Julie's method of relating to children is the preferred one.

Finally her camera flashes. Baldo runs toward the camera-shaped playhouse, and I have to drag him back. He back-dives, tantrums, screams as if he's being burned. He sinks his teeth into my shoulder. I put him down and begin talking to him calmly, holding his hands, trying to untantrum him.

Julie's beanie pops up over my shoulder. "Uh-oh! We've got a biter!"

I glare at her.

She breaks character. "That's, like, only the second biter I've had. He must be in daycare."

I'm going to strangle this woman with her rainbow suspenders. "No, he's at home with me."

"Did you teach him to bite?"

We struggle through the close-up.

"Let's talk props." Julie lobs the suggestion about the oversized Valentine's hearts.

"This may sound peculiar," I counter. "But do you have a broom?"

"A broom?" As if she's never heard of one.

"He really likes brooms," Jim explains. "It'll be fun for him."

Still her face is blank.

"You know, like in the back? For sweeping up?" I add.

"Well, yeah . . . I guess we have one. But it's not a *prop* broom."

"If he holds it, is it not a prop?" I wonder. This blows her mind for a minute.

"Wait!" she snaps her fingers. Julie is so smart! "There's a witch's broom for Halloween!" She returns with a child-size plastic broom.

Even the bristles are a solid mass of plastic. She hands it to Baldo, and he begins dragging it along the floor. He won't stand and pose with it.

The twins are still staring.

"This isn't working." I wrest the plastic broom out of Baldo's hand.

"Okay, we'll just go with those two shots." Julie is rejiggering her camera.

"No, this isn't *working*." I thrust the broom at her. "This environment is frustrating for toddlers. Are you sure we can't use one of the quieter rooms?"

"We have to use the front room first," she reiterates. "We can only use the back rooms if the front room is occupied."

"That's ridiculous. He's not going to just stand here while people are going by in front of him." School-age kids are scrambling past, gawking inside the photo studio.

I pick Baldo up, and we walk off. "Your pictures will be ready after noon!" Julie chirps.

We walk the entire length of the mall back to where we've parked.

"God, I hate this fucking place," Jim mutters.

"We're never coming back here," I agree in the elevator.

"Except to look at our pictures."

"Yeah."

We are all hungry and twenty minutes from home. We drive halfway back to eat at a restaurant that isn't a chain. Baldo tantrums in the chair.

I'm really sick of this crap, to the extent that it makes me want to smash shit up, and that's a big statement from someone who is easily placated by pie. I want to see a bunch of crazy parents dancing orgiastically around a bonfire of stupid prop hearts, oversized stars and moons, and industrial carpeting.

I'm going to put a sledgehammer through the window. I want to pull down and shatter all those stupid portraits on their walls— the ones with hapless infants strapped into angel wings; the ones with families all dressed alike, like they're starring in some kind of prime-time variety show from the 1970s with Harvey Korman. I want to grind all the fake, forced smiles into a thousand tiny pieces under the heel of my boot. All those generic faces, all those people wearing their cutest outfits from Old Navy, all the prints and package specials framed and hung on tasteful beige walls in McHouses from Scottsdale to Fort Myers. With the same couches and the same IKEA bin of LeapPad toys. All abiding by the same rules: Children must smile. We must not see the soles of their shoes. They must climb onto stepladders or big red wagons and be as whimsical as possible.

All this stuff is family-unfriendly. It's corporate-friendly. Why do we pump our money into this crap? Certainly we love our children. Why do we allow people in propeller beanies to torment them? Some of us know better. We skulked through high school in our Siouxsie t-shirts, refusing to smile when we weren't particularly happy; then we bred and some sleeper cell inside our brains activated, releasing a hormone that makes us disintegrate whenever Hanna Andersson has a sale. Striped tights! We must have striped tights!

What I'm really asking is this: Why is the mall where all the *families* are?

I saw all these mothers walking around with their babies in Pope-globe hermetic strollers. I had no idea there were so many other people with children in my town. I'd flag them down, but there's no place for us to stop and stand, to talk to one another. We're supposed to roam around like cattle, stopping only to buy or eat or piss.

It concerns me that for so many postpartum women walking around the mall with the baby is their way to "go out." Go out and what? Be isolated in public? Be surrounded by pictures of Abercrombie and Fitch models? Granted, when the four walls are closing in, anything is better than staying at home. But isn't there a better alternative?

I used to fantasize about a giant room with a soft, semi-padded floor, like a gym mat. A drain in the middle of the room to hose down the snot and graham cracker crumbs at the end of the day. You pay a buck or two to go inside with your baby. There are piles of toys, separated into different areas by age. You can plunk your three-month-old down on a playmat and sit and be among mothers. There'd be a coffeepot percolating in the corner, maybe some muffins that somebody brought in.

There will be no organized activities here. You will not be coerced into "circle time." The babies will not be made to play with scarves or clack claves along to some dorky music. And it is clear to all that *this is not exclusively for the benefit of your child.* This is not some shit to bring out your child's aptitudes or help her get into an exceptional preschool. This is because parenting is a group activity. We are not meant to be sectioned off into little dyads. We are supposed to interact and share our wisdom. We are meant to bitch to each other when we need it, to encourage each other when we need it. The very expression "Mommy and Me class" makes it clear that the baby is the subject and the mother the object.

For some parents, my dream is a reality. A friend who has recently moved to Hong Kong reports that her apartment complex has a "toddler room" for playtime. "Wow," she opines. "It's incredible. Padded floor and a baby ball pit. Lots of toys and books and tons and tons and tons of babies."

Other parents have told me about Family Place, a community center for families in Canada. One Vancouver location offers preschool activities, a toy library, parent support (including a home-visit service), and licensed "childminding" for kids eighteen months and over. The program receives government support from the city and from the Ministry for Children and Families, so admission costs 50¢. Fifty cents. Canadian.

"Family Place kicks ass," one parent told me. "It is one of the major things that I love about living here, that I think every neighborhood in the States could use."

This wouldn't fly in the United States. Not just because we do not mix government and parenting. More to the point is that we do not allow low-key, self-directed play. We have to make childhood as noisomely cheerful and strenuous as possible. Our "family restaurants" have to have birthday whistles and kiddie cups with licensed characters on them. We are—to quote a movie I recently reviewed—the "Fun Police." *If you aren't having fun, fun will be provided for you!* We can't allow our children to just sit there and stack blocks. We will regulate their activities so that every kid meets a Minimum Standard of Childish Glee. We will have DVDs in our minivans so that the ride from playgroup to Chuck E. Cheese is as *fun as possible!* Everything a child touches has to have at least one flashing light and beeping noise. You can't even have a plain toddler toothbrush. No, your toothbrush will be *fun!* With patented Fun Bristles™ and Fruit Berry Fun-sation training paste! The strawberries on the tube are smiling! Your diapers have smiling dinosaurs on the waistband! They're so happy to decompose and provide petroleum for your ass!

This shit exhausts me utterly. No wonder I'm medicated. Parenthood is the mass madness that childhood should be a big, giddy laugh riot; rather, it is complex and often frustrating to those who experience it. Childhood does not exist to look cute and move a product. Childhood is an end in itself.

Woe is you who venture outside of the officially sanctioned childhood spaces. People will look at you as if you've stepped out of a spacecraft with an extraterrestrial clutching your hand. *What is that . . . that small thing with her? Why is it so noisy? Can't she control it? It hurts my ears!* You will be deported to the McDonald's Play Place and made to genuflect before a giant corporate clown. You will eat food formed into nugget shapes. And you will like it, or else be cudgeled with a novelty diaper bag.

Where families cluster—those commuter neighborhoods—the big-box retailers follow. The organic full-fat baby yogurt they used to stock has been replaced with a brand with a Disney tie-in. It's got high fructose corn syrup, hydrogenated oils, and "poppin' color crystals™" that create a swirl effect. No more bland banana and vanilla—these come in Cotton Candy and Bubble Gum flavors. And there's a story—featuring a popular licensed character, of course—on the bottom of the lid! Another brand offers an "Orange Strawberry Banana Blowout." What used to be a starter food for kids trying out dairy now promises to be a complete multisensory experience, packed with as many flavors and action verbs as possible, lest we risk understimulating our children.

Must our yogurt be so amusing? No wonder our lives feel empty when we graduate to low-fat and all it has is a cow on the package.

To access the yogurt, you will run a gauntlet of greeters who make goofy faces at your toddler and possibly present him or her with a helium-filled balloon. If you are particularly unfortunate, your child will be latex-allergic and break out into a rash by the time you reach the dairy case. If you reject the balloon, your child's tearful wailing will echo from the tire shop to the photo lab. You have become the person you sneered at when you were young and single and knew everything. You are That Mother.

But it's not really your fault. You were doomed by the giant parking lot, the humming fluorescent lighting, the prominent placement of SpongeBob SquarePants, the giant, talking cardboard standees of NASCAR drivers. There is a conspiracy afoot; its purpose is to dope you and your child into grinning yourself to death. And you better smile, or else that feather duster's coming back.

HELL IS OTHER PARENTS

WHEN I WAS DOWN, I spent a lot of time comparing myself to other parents. It's just so easy to do. You get enough of us together in a room, and you realize we're all saying the same things. *No, honey, that's not for climbing. Can we put that back? Five more minutes, then it's time for lunch.* No one is saying, "I think *Closely Watched Trains* is the best film of the Czech New Wave." Our cars are full of crumbs and crap and toys. We are susceptible to jealousy and mania.

I lucked out in finding a group of other parents who were really cool. However, they made me annoyed with myself for being so vanilla. They said, "We don't throw rocks, sweetie," while making elaborate vegan meals with nutritional yeast, putting out zines, and wearing excellent novelty t-shirts from the thrift store. They operated home businesses in their garages, screenprinting and network consulting and cloth-diaper sewing. They took their kids to punk shows. They took their kids on tour and *played* punk shows. They had done drugs with rock stars. They had done naughty webcams. I know teenage mamas who raised kids alone and put themselves through college and *still* kicked ass and raised hell and rocked out and smoked weed and put out zines—stuff I wasn't even able to do sequentially over the course of my thirty years. I know a single mama of refluxing *twins*. I know a mama who essentially raised her screaming, squalling, refluxing, food-allergic infant while her husband was on tour with GWAR, performing as "Beefcake the Mighty." I'd inevitably compare myself to them. I'd feel like Susie Homemaker. I was leading a sheltered, pampered, boring existence.

But then I'd show up twenty minutes early at the playground and actually be there *with* the Susie Homemakers, whose socks and sweaters matched. Their diaper bags were made of real leather. They had highlights from the salon. They took spinning classes and went to Gymboree. They quilted. They went to book groups. Among them, I'd feel as if I'd just struggled up out of a ditch alongside the highway with my child in a duffle bag. They were so put together. They did Mommy and Me classes and had circle time. They weren't crazy and unshowered. Their kids were cleanly attired and verbal and so obviously happy—happier than mine, anyhow. Their houses probably weren't besmirched with dried-on baby oatmeal. They probably had sex with their partners. I was a fucking shitty mother.

Not since high school had I felt like such an amorphous blob of personhood. Who the hell was I, anyway?

In one of my odd moments I went to Quizilla, the online repository of personality quizzes, to find a test to help me define myself. Using the search term "mom," I found the following:

> Are you a dumbass like your boolashnaka momma?
> DID YOU FUCK MY MOM?
> Does your Mom suck like mine?
> How big is [sic] *your* moms [sic] tits?
> How Easy Is Your Mom?
> How Hot is Your Mom?
> is your mom evil?

What kind of pervert is your mom?

The classic MILF (Mother I'd Like to Fuck) question, answered at last. (I'm not one.) According to the last quiz, I'm a "diapered plushophile." (I had to ask.) On the other hand, I'm not evil, and if I were a TV mom, I'd be Sharon Osbourne.

Some of the other quizzes assessed the quality of my mothering based on whether I smoked crack or had multiple babydaddies. I did well on these, since the answers to both those questions are currently no. Still, it was kind of reassuring, in a way.

But none of it was helpful, so I came up with my own reductivist categorization scheme with which to pigeonhole myself and others. I've called each of them "mother" because I am lazy, but fathers, grandparents, and other loved ones can also be shoehorned into these categories.

Earthy Crunchy Granola Mother

Wears a WAHM-made nursing dress sewn from recycled fabric patches. Has goats. Unschools. The kids play with Waldorf dolls and homegrown organic vegetables. Sometimes they write and perform original plays about sustainable living. No vaccinations; homeopathic and herbal healing only. Microwave ovens and dental amalgam are evil tools of the patriarchy. Hand-expresses her breast milk and uses it to make yogurt. Births unassisted in the surf. Children are named Starr Hope and Papaya.

My score: LOW. The patron saint of the ECGM is MangoMama (a.k.a. Jennifer VanLaanen-Smit), natural-parenting guru and erstwhile domme of mangomama.org. The site mysteriously disappeared, fanning the flames of rumor. Did MangoMama really freak out, skip the islands, and flee to Japan with a lover? Somebody told me this at playgroup. I think we may be projecting our fantasies onto her.

Crazy Mother

Wears stained maternity panties and the tiara from her kid's toybox. Eats cabrito. Sends the kids to sea camp. The kids play with homemade rattles crafted from dried beans and empty bottles of Xanax. Vaccinates to meet sea camp regulations; self-medicates with cocktail of Infant Motrin, simethicone drops, and Maker's Mark. Food comes from the microwave at 7-11. Pumps and dumps after too many margaritas. Births in the hospital, picks up scrip for Paxil on the way home. Children are named Luvox and Celexa.

My score: HIGH. 'Nuff said.

Indie Mother

Wears skirt made from a purse; carries purse made from a skirt. Eats the most paradoxical of foods—vegan queso. Sends the kids to Reggio Emilia cooperative preschool; their classmates are the scions of "snorecore" bandmates, zinemakers, and licensed piercers.

The kids play with 7" records, skateboards, and self-published tomes on antiglobalism.

Vaccinates selectively; medicates with herbal salves obtained through craft swapping.

Food comes from the CSA market; children furtively trade their lunches for Ho-Hos.

Pumps milk and freezes it in reusable canvas bags that can be made into skirts after weaning. Births at home with midwife; swaps placenta for blank CDs. Children are named Bright Eyes and The Incredible Moses Leroy.

  My score: MEDIUM. I think about doing this stuff. But then I don't actually do it.

What to Expect When You're a Mainstream Mom

Wears pink t-shirt, plain white socks, and Keds™. Eats Doritos™ and drinks Diet Coke™. Sends the kids to Primrose Schools™. The kids play with LeapPads™ and Hasbro Bop Its™. Vaccinates according to the American Academy of Pediatrics guidelines. Also vaccinates for anthrax and ADHD. Food comes from McDonald's™ and Lunchables™. Doesn't like to take breasts out. Births in hospital with epidural and pedicurist. Children are named Jaden, Braeden, Traeden, and Grayden.

  My score: MEDIUM. Bop Its™ rule.

Sunday School Mom

Wears floral-print smock dress. Tends flock; likes ovine metaphors. Sends the kids to Mother's Day Out. The kids watch Veggie Tales videos and play with The Full Armor of God play sets (*Ephesians 6:13-18*). Vaccinates according to belief in faith healing. Food comes from the Lord, and we are thankful. Breastfeeding is either (1) part of God's miraculous plan or (2) brazen and sinful. Births in Catholic hospital with chaplain. Children are named Jacob, Isiah, Rachel, Neariah, and Barnabas.

My score: LOW. Though I had hepatitis in a Catholic hospital, and I really wanted to call the chaplain to talk about God. And can you believe I'd never even heard of the Armor of God toys? I thought *Armor of God* was that movie in which Jackie Chan fell off a cliff doing a stunt and had to have a plate put into his skull.

Free-Market Mom
Wears Nikes and American flag t-shirts made in Pakistan by "terrorists." Baby wears "patriotic" one-piece outfits from Old Navy, also made in Pakistan. Eats steak. Feeds the baby pureed steak. Sends the kids to KinderCare; owns stock, too. The kids play with Rescue Heroes and Monopoly. Vaccinates quarterly; owns pharmaceutical stock. Food comes from ConAgra; also owns stock. Feeds Similac™ and Pediasure™; owns stock in Abbott Laboratories. Adds steak to bottle. Births in private hospital with financial advisor. Children are named George, Nancy, Laura, Donald, Newt, and Wal-Mart.
My score: LOW. But don't tell my parents.

Needless to say—I hope—you've realized that these categories are all actually bullshit. This kind of thinking does nothing but divide parents and make us judge each other. Though I'm not kidding about the Real Armor of God stuff; it really exists. If your preschoolers are persecuting heathens with a jock's mare as part of their pretend play, I'm probably going to pick up my stuff and go to the other side of the playground. And if you introduce yourself to me by saying, "Nice to meet you! I'm a cloth-diapering, elimination-communicating, extended-breastfeeding, baby-wearing, noncircumcising, homeschooling, nonvaccinating, peaceful parent!" I might run away.

Remember: *You are not your parenting choices.*

The coolest parents I've met are the ones who explode these categories. I like people who blow my mind a little bit. When I first met my friend Michelle, she was wearing a broad-brimmed floppy hat with a pink grosgrain ribbon, and she was crafty, and she sewed, and she was a SAHM (Stay-At-Home-Mom) with two toddlers, and she sang in her church choir and was married to an accountant and drove a solid American car. She made her own baby slings. Of course my little brain started filling in the blanks: Calphalon cookware and free-market capitalism and a nice Christian upbringing. Pretty soon she was telling me about stripping in New Orleans and her coke-whore roommates and her half-finished chemistry degree and her first marriage to a comic artist. She was giving me recipes with quinoa and starfruit and teaching me all manner of stuff from her self-education. I'd write notes to myself on a memo pad—books to read about the history of the textile industry. Each time we'd talk politics, she'd sound a little bit more like a socialist. I got schooled.

Then there was the Baby Matinee at our local indie view-and-brew theater, which seemed to attract a lot of women with Jennifer Aniston hair and complicated stroller systems. They all knew each other and had babies the same age. I felt geeky and inferior, so of course I had to get a big bug up my ass about it.

"Come to the movies with me," I begged Aunt Erin. "We can give the Gymboree moms something to talk about."

"Okay," she agreed, being unemployed and accountable to no one on a Tuesday afternoon.

So we met up for a screening of *Punch-Drunk Love*, the P. T. Anderson comedy with Adam Sandler. I got there first. I parked Baldo on my lap in the back row and ordered an Italian soda.

Aunt Erin slid into the seat next to me. "Hi, honey," she said, smirking. Then, genuinely, she gave Baldo a squeeze and a kiss on the cheek. She held on to his hand. It was sweet.

We waited to see how many people turned around to check us out, Baldo and his two ostensible mommies. Maybe a couple of people.

"Wait . . . no. Nobody's looking," Erin observed.

It hit me. "Hey, for all we know they could all be lesbian parents. I don't see any dads." We looked around. No dads. And the Gymboree moms were kind of cute. Maybe they had it going on. It seemed like a sweet deal, actually. They could swap clothes and get the kids in a circle and sing "Wheels on the Bus." Load everybody into the Chevy Tahoe and take off for the park—you could probably get enough toddler seats in that thing to eliminate the need for two, or even three, smaller cars. Set up a creche for the babies, a fishbowl full of pacifiers, a drawer full of plain white socks. Bust out a giant box of Tampax the same time each month. Nobody needs the mini-pill or an IUD. I'm not saying it's perfection, but it sounded like a sweet deal.

"You're very judgmental, you know," The Good Therapist had pointed out one time. "Do you realize how critical you are of others? You think you're smarter than everyone else."

I tried to wuss out with my usual line, that I'm an editor and my job upon the earth is to ferret out incorrect typefaces and omissions and transpositions, to squeeze in substitutions and strike things that don't belong. But The Good Therapist had an answer for everything. "You don't have permission to edit people. They have to agree to it. Just as you've agreed to be analyzed. It's not my right to meet you at a party and analyze you, for example."

So maybe it's me.

But I suspect there are reasons why parents are particularly inclined to criticize, to draw comparisons and snicker. We see ourselves only in contrast to others. Our very young children give us no feedback about our performance, especially if they're fussy or sick. Their problems surpass the solutions on hand. We know only that we don't have the answers, that we cannot provide what our children seek. We have a very human need to see the result of our endeavors. If our children do not reflect our success with their satisfaction and contentment, we'll find it by tearing down someone else. We'll find it by slagging somebody who couldn't manage to wash cloth diapers, who wasn't successful at breastfeeding. We'll criticize a parent who uses a portable infant seat instead of a soft carrier. We'll criticize someone who doesn't play Mozart for the baby. We'll criticize someone who doesn't play The Damned for the baby. We'll call a homebirther a hippie freak; we'll assume a caesarean mother wasn't educated about her choices, was induced too soon by a pushy doctor and Failed to Progress.

I once watched some users on a playgroup listserv go gaga over someone's lotus birth. That's cool and all, but you're not going to get a prize. I respect the natural birth movement, but not to the extent of lionizing mothers who birth "peacefully" and shoving all the others into a pile. I also watched a new user introduce herself thus:

> When I do have children I plan to give birth unassisted, breastfeed, use elimination communication, not vaccinate, eat organic, use slings, home school, and basically bring my children up the best I can.

I'm very happy for her—truly, I am—but I don't ever, ever want to meet this person. The last organic thing I ate was an Amy's micro-wave burrito, and I stood way too close to the oven while it was nuking. My version of elimination communication is muttering obscenities while Baldo waters the carpet during Naked Time. I use hideous plastic diapers filled with some kind of space-age super-absorbent gel. I pump my kid full of antihistamines and cover him with steroidal ointments tested on lab rabbits by evil pharmaceutical corporations; then I read *The Pudgy Bunny Book* to my child without irony. Yet I too believe that I'm bringing my child up the best I can, and anyone who argues with that can just kiss my *yoni*.

Wait—one more example that really got under my skin: a screen-printed romper with a squalling kid on it and the legend: "CRYING IT OUT? PICK ME THE &#$* UP!" First of all, if you don't have the eggs to say "fuck," don't even start to play that game with me. Secondly, I'm all about the whimsical babywear, and I'm cool with using my kid as a sandwich board for my own opinions. Babies do so little. Why not use them for advertising space? However, there's a subtle difference between, say, a "fuck off" to a public figure and a message that singles out other parents, different parents, for rebuke. If you want to be a warrior for your parenting style—which I think is kind of messed up, but let's just say—you might start by fighting the real enemy: one of the celebrity gurus making money off his or her library of childcare dogma. You have no idea whether the mother who sees that shirt and blushes and gulps is a single mother of refluxing twins or the wife of Beefcake the Mighty. Unless you came to my house and rocked my son during one of his massive scream-a-thons, you don't get to judge me.

Everybody makes plans for our children that don't come to pass. The sad thing is when we beat ourselves up over it. The sadder thing is when we beat each other up for it.

THE PARENTS WE ARE
AND THE PARENTS WE WISH WE WERE

I BECAME PREGNANT during the initial groundswell—to my knowledge, anyway—of "hip" parenting as a zeitgeist. You could be a mother and still be yourself. You could still play pedal steel in a punkabilly band; you could still wear Fluevogs and color your hair purple. You can wear your baby in a Maya Wrap while you're culture jamming on Buy Nothing Day or screaming animal-liberation epithets into the drive-through speaker at Bill Miller BBQ. In fact, it's good to do these things: Our subsequent generations won't feel the pressure to conform, to choose between their personal passions and their love for their families.

I still think it's a great idea—in theory. I was raised by a mother who was pressured away from her studies as an artist by a sexist college advisor. Primary education was a much more seemly vocation for Woman; it didn't dry up her uterus like turkey jerky or cause prolapse, and it could be laid aside or resumed, according to the needs of her children. So my mother obtained a teaching certificate and used it until my sister was born. When we began half-day kindergarten, the house began to fill with "projects": those strange creations born of the union of the artistic impulse and homemaking. My mother kicked ass at crafts. First it was pastels. Then ceramic painting and gold-leafing. This was not art. This was domestic beautification. I'm well aware of the movement to reclaim "women's arts"—quilting and scrapbooking and the like—as artistically legitimate, and that's cool. But potholders and waist-high ceramic giraffes were not my mother's métier. She'd preferred abstract expressionism and had been celebrated for her sculptures, created by squeezing the clay in anger. The clay took squat, bulbous shapes—tree stumps, shameful homunculi with Jimmy Durante noses—upon which the viewing mind could impose all sorts of protofeminist flights of fancy. My mother never complained, but the tiny critic of the house (i.e., me) was not inspired by the jewelry keepers she made from school boxes with our Girl Scout troop.

So when the time came for me to spawn, I was drawn to mothers who appeared to kick ass in their antepartum manner. Playing bagpipes. Drawing cartoons about liberation theology.

Wearing thigh-high boots and aviator's caps. What could be more wonderful than to be an infant, strapped to the strong, proud body of a badass mama—someone political and interesting and culturally literate? A fighter for justice and peace and human rights? A nurturer who'll flip off anyone who gets in her face about nursing in public, refusing vaccinations, birthing at home? A maternal avenger?

Cut to me, at home with a newborn. I'd envisioned myself tucked contentedly in my nursing station: the IKEA rocker, nutrition bars and water at my side, my sweet, pacific baby in my arms while I listened to *All Things Considered* and pondered the evils I would vanquish for my son and all children (the flat tax, standardized testing in our schools, mercury in groundwater). But that wasn't quite the reality. Instead, I was eating a microwave burrito and watching *Montel* with the captions on. And I was a long way from gallivanting around in my snakeskin-print pleather flares. I wasn't even sure where they were.

I'd fallen into the trap so many parents (but women, particularly) lay for themselves these days: I idolized parents who showed *no signs of actually being parents.* At least no signs apparent to me—maybe that's the important distinction to be made. Their parenting was invisible to the casual observer. Everything appeared effortless. When they wrote about the travails of parenthood in their soy-ink zines or complained—as did Kate Winslet—about diapering in interviews with *Vanity Fair,* even *that* was effortless. Your value as a person depended on what you managed to do in spite of being a mother.

Maybe I was stuck in some kind of hipness trap (which is funny, because I'm about as hip as a Kansas City reference librarian), but there are other kinds of pitfalls. *My body will go back exactly the way it was. Of course we'll still have sex when we're parents! My kid will not wear something like that. I'm not going to carry a bag with bunnies on it, unless a bunny is the new Gucci logo. I'm still going out to shows. We are not watching* Barney *in this house.*

But the truth is you will become the parent you are, and who knows what that is? Perhaps you will do inconceivably dorky things. Perhaps you will begin wearing puce polyvinyl pants instead of tasteful separates from Petite Sophisticate because they are more vomit-repellent. Perhaps you will outgrow your DIY Tank Girl t-shirts when your milk comes in, and you will wear periwinkle cotton nursing sweaters because your next-door neighbor gives them to you and they're comfortable and free of charge. Perhaps you will set aside your cherished avocations (transsexual fetish photography, herotica, competitive checkers); perhaps you will discover new ones. Perhaps you will become a single parent if you are partnered; perhaps you will become partnered and suburban and domestic after all if you are single. Perhaps your great-aunt will break her hip and come live with you, displacing your life partner's klezmer bandmates, who've been crashing in your guest room, and you will turn around twice and find yourself the very model of unpaid domestic caregiving, and you will scream and cry and go to bed at seven every night from sheer exhaustion.

Who gives a fuck? You'll do what you can.

See, the problem as I see it isn't you or me, or the low-grade celebrity mothers (usually soap stars) who are smiling from the covers of pregnancy magazines whose writers gush, "But how do you manage to *do it all?*"

The problem is that phrase exactly: "doing it all." It's a losing proposition, and becoming worse. In other words, how do you manage to keep your motherhood so secret that, if it weren't for the title of the magazine and the little rosy-cheeked toddler next to you, there would be no evidence that you were a mother at all? You're not fat and tired; you don't have visible roots in your hair and crushed Goldfish crackers stuck to your ass. Hipness can be another kind of trap, our expectations just as repressive.

Too often, we live in houses that are far away from our town centers and places of employment. We don't know our neighbors. We commute upon and down freeways, stopping at neat and self-contained supermarkets if we need anything (and we always do, don't we?). Our children attend childcare centers or stay at home with us. Either way, they're cordoned off from the rest of the world. We are compartmentalized. We are isolated. So isolated that Montel's voice is a comfort.

How I wished to be vibrant and active, like a Zapotec woman with a colorful *rebozo* and a stall in the market square for onions and chayote squash. The children could count change and all play together, and then we'd have our seasonal fiesta. People with alternative lifestyles would be embraced and celebrated as shamans.

I wanted to be a parent whose kid wore whimsical novelty t-shirts. Whimsical novelty t-shirts are a way of life in Austin. You can be ironic (a vintage concert tee from Styx's *Kilroy Was Here* tour) or DIY or in your face. You can distress and reconstruct. You can put UPC numbers or binary code on your torso. In Austin, it is cool to have a Bedazzler. Your t-shirt will proclaim your sexuality, your political affiliations, your ZIP code. All of these whimsical novelty t-shirts are freakin' adorable on children.

I melted all over a commemorative toddler tee from South by Southwest—the music, film, and multimedia festival held in town each year. On it a sock monkey in headphones spun records on two turntables. It cost $15—the most I'd ever spent on a single item of children's clothing. I imagined Baldo cavorting in it at the coffee shop, chasing kickballs in the park. Hardened hipsters would weep. *That kid's parents must be good, good people. Why, they're so cool, they're hardly parents at all.* When I got home from my assigned screenings to a tearful Baldo—who misses me when I'm out being an international cinema journalist—I presented it to him.

"Isn't it great?" I prompted.

He opened his mouth wide and wailed. "The monkey doesn't love me!"

"Oh, sure it does, honey! He wanted me to bring him home so he could hug you!"

"I don't like it I don't like it I don't like it! That is a scary monkey!"

Scary monkey? Nothing about my son suggested a fear of monkeys—not the way he danced to "Hockey Monkey" by James Kolchaka Superstar or "Abba Dabba Honeymoon," not the way he loved for me to pick him up under my arm and lug him around as if I were a mother gorilla, not his Curious George books, not our Barrel of Monkeys game—nothing.

"Make the monkey go away!"

The shirt his grandmother sent him? With dump trucks? Yeah, he loves that. The UT football shirt his dad got him? Loves that. Uh-huh. He likes the motorcycle-print footies from Baby Gap more than the gorgeous pajamas our friend Justine sent from Hong Kong. (Won't even try them on.) And it's not because he's a "boy's boy" or any shit like that. He's just determined to confound every expectation.

By the by, I've heard people get bent out of shape over the phenomenon of "cool" kidswear, as if we're turning our kids into whimsical indie fashion accessories, like knitted cell-phone cozies and Neighborhoodies. No worse, I'd argue, than making him pose for portraits with a miniature football or stuffing a little tomboy into a tea-party dress. You're giving up enough of your personality as it is. Your kid isn't going to suffer because you made him a bootleg Ween shirt. You should see the fashion atrocities I survived as a preschooler in the early 1970s. My clothes had stoplights and disco slogans on them: NO PARKING ON THE DANCE FLOOR! People probably thought it was hilarious to put us in itty-bitty doubleknits with butterfly collars. My sister and I had matching ensembles culled from the two predominant trends in 1970s girlswear: sack dresses inspired by *Little House on the Prairie* and shiny satin short-shorts reminiscent of coke binges behind the velvet rope at Studio 54. No one ever asked us what we thought about it.

Making cultural choices as a parent is like any other part of the task. Do what you do, and don't hurt yourself trying. You haven't failed if you're not the coolest parent on the block. If you break down and buy the green gel soap that squirts out of Shrek's ears instead of using vegan cleansers with organically grown essential oils made by hand at the co-op. If your kid refuses to wear plaid punk pants and tiny Chuck Taylor All-Stars. I've seen nothing lovelier in my life than pictures of Stephen Egerton, the bald and seemingly scary guitarist for Descendents, having a "princess party" with his three-year-old daughter. She's put a tiara on him. It'll make you cry, man.

I was not a Maternal Avenger. Curiously, I looked to motherhood to make me hipper than I already was. What the fuck was I thinking? I'll admit I was impressed with myself when I scored a pair of retro zebra-print cotton pegged pants at Goodwill for $1.99. When I dressed Baldo in them and took him out on the town, a guy on a cell phone actually stopped his conversation to say, "Dude, I wish you could see this kid's pants! He looks like he's in Pat Benatar's *band* or something." That was fun. Let's be honest.

But I compromised, too. I did a lot less writing than I thought I would—I was too busy walking the floor. Even after the reflux and the eczema and the colic and the depression lifted, I still sat around a lot playing Candy Land, while my brain was so desperate for creative stimulation that I thought quite seriously about writing a film adaptation of the game. (Michael "The Commish" Chiklis would star as Gloppy, the lovable molasses monster more "goosome" than "gruesome.") As a writer, I had never been more motivated but less able to work. It was torturous. I watched fewer movies than ever before. I'd rent movies when they came out, already six months behind everyone else, and I'd still crash on the couch after taking a bath with Baldo and diapering him and putting on his jammies and nursing and reading three stories from *Richard Scarry's Great Big World of Whatever* and singing two songs and giving goodnight kisses and cleaning up the kitchen and putting all the bath toys away and wiping up. I couldn't write any year-end "best of" lists. And yet I was fantastically grateful that it was better, that I was better, that Baldo was better, that our marriage was better, and that my mental health was better. Still, I was furiously envious of any parent who managed to do something even halfway cool.

Some mornings I would wake up with the itch to create. I'd have an idea for a short story, for a feature, for a column. Sometimes I'd dream up the conclusion to a piece I'd been working on for months, and in the half-remembered haze of waking to my child's cries, I'd yell for the dozing Jim to bring me a Post-it and a pen so I could scribble something, *anything* about it while I was nursing. The next day I could hardly read what I'd jotted. I'd long so badly to sit at my desk and write, uninterrupted, for even an hour—I'd be shaking with resentment while I rolled out Play-Doh or gritted my teeth through *A Surprise for Thomas* "one more time." On these days, it meant a lot to me to have that bootleg Ween shirt, to have a KISS patch sewn over the cutesy juvenile logo on my microfiber baby backpack. *I am still here*, I'd think. It meant a lot that I could crank up a mix CD I made for the two of us, that I could listen to Junior Brown and Red Foley instead of Raffi. (These are just my personal preferences, culturally. If you honestly like Raffi, rock on.) It meant that I was not entirely on the shelf. I had not reduced myself to a mommy-shaped container of nurturance.

Depressed people often fear our personalities will evaporate when we are healed, that we will no longer be charismatic, tragic superstars, or that medication will zombify us into blandness and passivity. Depressed mothers really get the double whammy. We're supposed to express sheer delight with our children's every utterance and play along animatedly for hours. We're supposed to get really excited over songs about herbivorous dinosaurs that are set to the tune of "This Old Man." We're not allowed to be curmudgeonly anymore; chances are that was a big part of our self-concept to begin with.

Yet I was going to get out of this mothering thing not only alive, but with my personality intact. It could actually happen with slow, steady steps. Other mothers were in fact racing past me—playing roller derby and being Radical Cheerleaders—but I was on the path just the same. As my son became more verbal and expressive, he even seemed to appreciate the nuances of my personality. I could crack a corny joke and make him smile. I could get him to dance to Prince and Pizzicato Five. I could take him thrift shopping. At last I had a sense of our family's own unique character. It healed me.

I also discovered that I'd been fooling people after all with my "fake it until you make it" philosophy. Not that it was really important to fool people—it was better to just be honest with myself. Nonetheless, it amused me when I visited the newspaper office for a conference with my new editor, who followed me down the hall and admired the punk paraphernalia on my diaper bag.

"Well, you know," I demurred. "I can't handle how homogenizing motherhood is. Culturally."

"You seem to be doing okay with it," he offered.

Really? The last time we'd met in person, I'd run into him at the neighborhood supermarket months ago. He was shopping for hangover remedies, and I was standing, tear-streaked, in the cereal aisle during a four-alarm PPD freakout, Jim and Baldo waiting at home. My editor had to wave his hand in front of my face to get my attention and re-introduce himself to me; that's how out of it I was. I think I'd been trying to decide whether I should abandon my half-full cart and go crash the Volvo.

Now I'm pretty glad I checked out my groceries and came home.

PARENTAL ADVISORY

I GUESS I JUST ASSUMED that babies never grow up to understand words besides "bird" and "cup." But here was ours at fifteen months, trying out a phrase we were bandying about at breakfast. *"Buh pluh,"* he said. We looked at each other.

"Did you just say 'butt plug'*?"* Jim asked.

"Buh pluh." Baldo smiled.

A month later, I was toweling off after a morning shower. Jim stuck his head in the door.

"Hey, I got that talking caterpillar to say 'fuck,'" he beamed. We'd been trying for months to coax vulgarities out of Alphabet Pal, that purple plastic rolling caterpillar who sings out ostensibly educational noises. You can put it on the phonics setting and push the A and S keys in rapid succession, for example, but the little shithead giggles and says, "That tickles!" Surely we could trick it. At last we had.

I'm not saying any of this is a good idea, though I think Alphabet Pal is taking things a little too far. (It's not as if you push a series of buttons and it plays "Cop Killer.") It's just so difficult for us to always be appropriate. My mother, who had to stop watching *The Sopranos* due to the "blue" language, was horrified to learn that during our colic phase, we developed the habit of soothing the baby with the old *Saturday Night Live* chestnut "I'm Gonna Get Me a Shotgun and Kill All the Whiteys I See." Remember that one? Garrett Morris? He's gonna get him a white woman wearing a navy blue sweater? Anyhow, we reached a point where we couldn't think of anything else to sing, and here it came, bubbling up out of our long-term memories, and it worked like a charm. But then you reach the point where your child can say "butt plug," and you start to reconsider saying all the weird shit you're thinking.

Sometimes when I'm reading Richard Scarry's *What Will I Wear Today?* out loud, I find myself mentally adding different scenarios for Huckle and Lowly and their friends. Instead of, "What will I wear to play sports?" I wonder, "What will I wear to Sally's Dungeon?" Let's say that Sally, a femdom, has two submissives: Pig Will and Pig Won't. Pig Will is compliant and loves to please Sally. He craves humiliation (Pig Will really is such a squarejohn, isn't he?). So maybe his accessories are a scrub brush for Sally's bathroom, a can of Bon Ami, saddle shoes, a small O-ring gag, a metal plate collar, and a package of adult diapers. Pig Won't is a rebellious slave and needs firmer discipline. Should he wear the full hood? The suspension cuffs? The fur blindfold today? I seriously think about this stuff. I'm kind of a sick puppy.

The good news is that after months of practice, you can *think* inappropriate thoughts while *reading* appropriately. It's kind of a neat trick. Thanks to parenthood, I could probably plan out a full-on play party for Bob the Builder and Wendy in my head while carrying on a conversation about something radically different: herb gardening, dental hygiene, intellectual history. In other words, you can act like June Cleaver and think like Susie Bright. It's quite a bit of fun, really.

Here's another example: *Blue's Clues*. Let me remind you that I started out strenuously antitelevision. We watched nothing for the first two years, not even when I had hepatitis and spent several days at home on the floor, grunting with pain. I was still trying to play peek-a-boo and establish the concept of object permanence while my liver was exploding out of my body. Finally Baldo gave up his naptime at two-and-a-half, and I was desperate to introduce a sedentary, calming activity that didn't involve reading *Miffy's Magnifying Glass* eleven times. So it was on to tapes of *Blue's Clues* after lunchtime. I doled out episodes parsimoniously—one per day—from the tapes I got at a secondhand children's store. And I began to understand why I'd heard women on parenting boards fantasizing about ramming the original host, Steve Burns, with a green striped *buh pluh*. Those soulful brown eyes, the unselfconscious way he sings "The Mail Song." According to an interview in *Spin*, Steve, who left the show to pursue a career in quirky indie rock, has the original "thinking chair" in his bedroom, and his lady friends are after him to "do it" (his term) in the chair. "I'd feel like I was having sex in front of a million parents," he explained. That's a bad thing?

After we started watching the show, Baldo started putting "clues" on everything in the house, including my butt. Jim and I would exchange glances and chuckle. Then he put a "clue" on Jim's pant leg one morning at breakfast.

"What does Blue want to do with a pant leg?" I asked. We exploded into laughter.

"Wait, wait! Here's one. Now, our first clue is this *mirror.* And our second clue is this *razor blade.* And our third clue is this *straw.* What does Blue want to do with a mirror, a razor blade, and a straw?"

During long and napless afternoons, we'd meddle with the "Create a Word" game on Baldo's LeapFrog Phonics Writing Desk™. *"WOW!"* it cried. "You can write your *own* three-letter word. When you're finished, press the letters to spell out your word!"

We looked at each other.

It egged us on. "Write *any* three-letter word."

Any?

A-S-S didn't work. Neither did F-U-K. The LeapFrog Phonics Writing Desk™ just repeated its spiel.

S-O-D.

"Sod," it said. "Great job!"

Of course, our tomfoolery started catching up with us. I took Baldo to play with the train table at a bookstore, and he shyly edged up among the kids already scooting the engines around the tracks. Their parents—shorts-and-a-belt types talking about Mother's Day Out—seemed to look askance at me a little; maybe it was my imagination. At first.

Baldo began to sing a song from the CD I'd been playing in the car, an '80s mix.

"Are you ready for the sex girls?" he queried.

I gagged on my nicotine-replacement gum and bounced up from the bench.

"*Six* girls?" I blurted, overeager. "Do you see *six* girls? Let's count! One, two . . ."

He didn't hear me. "Sex, sex, sex, sex!" he trilled—the bridge from "Are You Ready for the Sex Girls?" by Gleaming Spires.

We didn't stay long after that.

Then there was the time at the sandbox in our park. Baldo was sharing his excavator and dump truck with a younger girl from the neighborhood.

"I like the way you shared that truck with her," I narrated. Not praise, just positive parenting. The other mom smiled.

"Girl!" Baldo shouted suddenly.

She straightened up.

"I wanna take you to a GAY BAR, GAY BAR, GAY BAR! Weeeeooow!" He air-guitared the solo from "Gay Bar" by Electric Six.

Not long after that incident I went to the holiday party thrown annually by the *Austin Chronicle*, for which I write movie reviews. I drank a lot of wine—I was by myself and had a designated driver meeting me later—and I repeated these stories to three or four different groups of people. Nobody seemed terribly bothered. One person got up to go share the story.

Later one of the other film contributors passed by me, new boyfriend in tow. They were on their way out the door to go see Magnetic Fields, whose songs include "How Fucking Romantic" and "Let's Pretend We're Bunny Rabbits."

She introduced me to her date.

"I've seen your byline," he said politely. Minor spark of recognition.

"Marrit's the 'butt plug' mom," she added.

"Oh, *right!* Butt plug, yeah."

"We were just talking about that. See you later."

Once when I told the stories, the listener, a Montessori teacher, asked me, "Do you think he's gay?"

"Baldo?"

"Yeah."

I thought about it. "He's two years old. I don't know if he's anything yet." I considered the question for a while. He didn't seem to possess any of the traditionally feminine characteristics we associate with scaring homophobic parents shitless. He didn't nurture. He did like to play with my lipstick, but he usually just ate it. Then I remembered something.

"He has a Little Tykes tool bench, but he takes the bins out of the bottom, puts them on his feet, and pretends he's ice skating to Bronski Beat."

"I see."

"Yeah."

"Would it bother you?"

"Of course not. I just want him to respect himself and other people, I suppose."

"You'd be surprised how many parents would be afraid of that."

"Really?" Of all the things a parent has to worry about? I reflected on my various concerns: toxic levels of mercury in the tuna-fish sandwiches, the traffic on our street, the stray chow chow who wandered into our yard, peanut-induced anaphylactic shock.

Then I started to realize that I really don't care about sexual explicitness. When we drove by graffiti of a giant penis on the side of a warehouse, Baldo and I both busted up laughing. "That penis is going pee-pee!" he hooted. We made the block to see it again. I worry about the Super Soaker that found its way into the toy chest at the coffeehouse more than I worry about "Gay Bar." The first time my kid asks about sex, I'm probably going to bore him with too much detail. I have visions of myself interrogating high school girlfriends (or boyfriends, I guess): "Do you kids have a 'safe word'? If your relationship is fluid bound, you really need to use a barrier, okay, sweetie? Wait! Where are you going? I'm about to make popcorn!"

ME **AGAINST THE MUSIC**

WITH THE BABY SCREAMING in my arms, I couldn't reach our CDs. Jim had tucked them away, alphabetized and filed in plastic sleeves, behind childproof doors at the bottom of our built-in shelves. It was a good idea at the time and probably would be again later, when youthful hands yearned to fling our music collection hither and yon.

The shelves at my level held our treasury of tapes from my own musical Camelot—Robyn Hitchcock and the Egyptians, Smithereens, XTC, Jane's Addiction, Billy Bragg, The Pixies, The Smiths, Smashing Pumpkins' *Gish*. Some had been replaced on CD; some languished, forgotten (Teenage Fanclub, The Wonder Stuff), after we moved into our house two years ago.

Around the clock I'd scramble through the cupboard with one hand, supporting the baby—in the crook of my elbow or the sling—in the other. I'd reach in blindly and pull out something, anything. Ancient mix tapes from ancient ex-boyfriends. Fuzzy, gnarly tapes worn thin from recording and re-recording. Freebie tapes from my job with an entertainment distributor. Compilations I'd started and forgotten Back in the Day. *Meet the Beatles*.

I'd stick a tape in our player and begin my endless routine of dancing with the baby. I danced the baby in the morning. I danced the baby at night. All night. I danced the baby in the afternoon. If I was lucky, he fell asleep and I could ease myself down into our rocking chair and keep the motion going. Sometimes I'd turn off the stereo with the remote and try to content myself with morning television with the sound off and the closed captions on. Sometimes I could ease him, sling and all, into the bassinet, and he might just stay asleep there for fifteen or twenty minutes. I'd lower him down a millimeter at a time, counting in my head: *One thousand one, one thousand two, one thousand three.* After a minute I'd start to slip my hands out from under him. Slowly. *One thousand one, one thousand two.* If he started to squirm, I'd pull out one hand and lay it on top of him until he settled. Then I'd raise one finger at a time from him. *One thousand one, one thousand two.* When the last finger was gone and I was no longer touching him, I'd begin to stand back up. Slowly. *One thousand one, one thousand two.* Sometimes it worked. Usually he felt me withdraw from him, and I'd have to gather him, both of us now crying, back up to my chest and begin again.

Sometimes I couldn't take the uncertainty, so I'd stay in the chair and rock him for however long the nap lasted. My head was full of everything and nothing. The tapes would play back to front, front to back on auto reverse, endlessly. I'd listen to a single album all afternoon, sometimes all day. The words and music were my companions. *Ballet for a rainy day / Silent film of melting miracle play / Dancing out there through my window / To the backdrop of a slow descending grey.* I cried sometimes. Sometimes I sat in a dull stupor, hardly aware that I was rocking. Sometimes I remembered a moment, a thought, something associated with a certain chord progression, a certain turn of phrase. I remembered the stuttering engine of a Volkswagen Beetle driven by a friend of a friend to a party where I drank too much and had to pee outside in the yard, a neighbor's dog barking at me. I remembered reading *Middlemarch*. I remembered the time I had the stomach flu and took a tranquilizing anti-emetic syrup from a health clinic; I lay in bed woozily, half-asleep with My Bloody Valentine on auto-repeat. I'd been trying to compile an annotated bibliography about the My Lai massacre, and the curves and straights of a book's typeset letters made me feel swervy. I gave up and let the music wash me back and forth in my bed. I propped my head on the sill of my window on the third floor of my dormitory, the same one my great-aunt Thyra had lived in forty years earlier when she went to the same college. Our floor was said to be haunted by the ghost of a "house mother" from long ago. Now the music washed me back and forth in my own house, sitting in a chair with a baby bound to my chest, and my great-aunt Thyra was home in Madisonville, Texas, dying of pancreatic cancer. We wanted her to meet the baby, but the four hours of driving were prohibitive for me. But I was always moving in place or in an elliptical orbit around my living room furniture.

"God, and that's all the most depressing music, too," Jim noted.

The music was my only connection to the person I used to be, a person I no longer was. During one long, agonizing evening, Jim took our tax return to an accountant for preparation; the deadline was looming, and everything had to go on in spite of the baby.

"Are you going to be okay here by yourself?" he'd asked, gathering up all of our paperwork and reaching for his keys.

"No." But there wasn't any alternative. Yet I wouldn't lie. He wasn't entitled to peace of mind if I never had it.

I nursed the baby, and he twisted and screamed, threw up. Screamed. Screamed. I dug in the cabinet, and my fingers grazed *Pretty Hate Machine* by Nine Inch Nails. My best friend from high school gave it to me our senior year, in early 1990. Someone— probably me—had sat on the case at some point, so it practically fell open my hand. It was perfect. It was primal and petulant, with layers of thudding, repetitive beats and bleeps, and I bounced the baby up and down against my body to them while my other hand tapped in time on his back, as if trying to reach through his skin and regulate his body from the inside out. An hour passed without a break in the baby's crying. The fuzzy guitar finish of "Ringfinger" came and went. The phone rang, and I sobbed into the cordless extension. "He won't stop crying. He won't stop crying." Jim had questions about our deductions.

"Are you listening to Nine Inch Nails? God, Marrit, why are you listening to that?"

What should I have listened to? *Baby Mozart?* Music that was strange to me, that was never part of who I was, that was for the baby? Everything was for the baby. Everything I ate or didn't eat. Every movement of my body, from the slow withdrawal of my fingertips from his fitfully sleeping back to every step I took around my living room, was for the baby. My body was now alien to me, devoted to his purposes. The angry red slash across my slackened belly. The dull pain of my incision replaced by numbness. Where the nerves had been severed I could poke my abdomen and sense nothing, as if I were touching another person. Now I couldn't feel except to press bitter little half-moons into my palms with my fingernails. Except to slip the nail clippers away from the baby in my lap—I had to cut his nails short when he slept so he wouldn't scratch the bumps and sores of his eczema—and close the cold little blades around some part of myself that was fleshy and exposed, within reach, available for injury. A pain that was not for the baby but was selfishly my own.

Better that, as I danced and rocked and consoled, I heard words I knew, words that made sense to me now.

When I was too tired to walk, we'd go out for drives before sunrise, trolling the neighborhood for solace, listening to my used-bookstore copy of *The Downward Spiral*. When I was too tired to drive, I'd park the wagon in the lot of the Methodist church where my son, years later, would eventually attend preschool. A mother-shaped thing behind the wheel cried while her son struggled wakefully in his car seat. Surely they wouldn't force me out of here. They have to help me. If there is a God, someone will come out and help me. They will know. Someone has been here before, parked in her car, slipping away from what she used to be while sitting in place.

> It won't give up it wants me dead
> Goddamn this noise inside my head

It meant something real to me to hear words put to this maelstrom of feelings. To have something crafted from madness implied a reason beyond it, a purposefulness I could regain somehow. Something inside me was capable of creation, of explication. If I felt the desire to obliterate myself, stronger than the urge to vomit, I could separate it from me by naming it. There was a self inside me that was not sick, that could reason.

And I began to write.

KID **ROCK**

"WE'RE NOT GOING TO LISTEN to kids' music," Jim had asserted when I was pregnant.

"We'll listen to a little of everything," I agreed.

"Kids' music is okay if it's cool," he affirmed.

"Cool like *Free to Be You and Me?*"

"Yeah, like that. Except, you know, *cooler.*"

"Right. Yeah. We're definitely going to do that."

"We're going to listen to our music."

"Yeah."

"Yeah."

When I was a child in the 1970s—a time of ever so many benevolent lies—it was all just music, suitable for everyone. Everybody soft-pedaled everything. We had songs about drugs and sex and urban riots. Yet they were so cheerful and goofy about it. I mean, there are a hundred dead police officers in Paper Lace's "The Night Chicago Died." I watched Diana Ross perform "Love Hangover" on *The Muppet Show,* flanked by giant, squiggly Muppets who looked like marabou boas. It was no big deal, somehow. I can remember riding to my grandmother's house, listening to "Afternoon Delight" by The Starland Vocal Band, thinking it was some horrible song about a picnic with fireworks. Everything was on a need-to-know basis.

But let's just say that the music in my adult collection is not particularly coy.

"The lyric thing is getting to be a problem," a friend of mine confessed. "I was zoning out driving a while back, and then realized my kid was singing along to Ween, 'Don't shit where you eat.'"

"This happened to us too!" another person piped up. "But it was 'wavin' my dick in the wind'!"

I'm not trying to be censorious. It's great to sing about your nads. But when your toddler runs around in public parroting remarks about having his dick out in the wind, you imagine the CPS caseworker sneaking up behind you, scribbling furiously. Some people believe children have *no curiosity* and *no awareness* about their nether realms unless there's been adult interference. No need to ratchet up your Parent Stress Quotient unnecessarily. It also concerns me when my kid screams for '*poon*'—by which, of course, he means '*a spoon.*'

Nor did our child necessarily appreciate our music—a common enough pitfall for parents. Why, I remembered rolling around the Houston suburbs as a child, belted into our brown-on-brown custom van with Don Williams in the 8-track player, crooning "I Believe in Love." How could I have known that, twenty-five years later, I'd be nostalgic for my father's vintage torch-and-twang?

My sister and I misheard the lyrics to George Jones's "He Stopped Lovin' Her Today."

"They placed a ring upon his dog?" she asked. "Why would they do that?"

"They placed a *wreath* upon his *door*," Dad corrected.

"Is it Christmas?" I wondered.

"No. He's dead. Soon they'll carry him to his grave. That's why he stopped loving her."

We went silent.

"Can we put on ABBA?" she asked.

One of my first victories as a parent was Black Sabbath. I was exhausted and medicated, so I began lifting the baby over my head and intoning, "*I am Iron Man!*" I'd plop him on the couch and stagger across the room, Ozzy-like, trailing my arms behind me for our mutual amusement.

It stuck. When Baldo was old enough to speak, he'd pipe, "Iron man!" in his little toddler falsetto. He'd sing the riff. I wept tears of joy and blogged furiously. We even convinced him that if he ate enough lima beans, he would transform *into* Iron Man, replete with heavy boots of lead. Then I explained that Iron Man doesn't really need "vengeance from the grave." He can use his words!

"Are you doing any kind of music classes?" asked our friend Mark, who's kind of a corporate fast-tracker, whereas I am from the Planet of Slack.

"We're learning 'Iron Man'!" I beamed. He gave me a funny look. I get a lot of those.

"I'm going to teach you how to rock," I told Baldo one morning over cereal. If children were taught from birth how to rock, they could rock *twice* as hard by the time they became rebellious adolescents, having mastered the fundamentals of rocking!

I'd pegged him as a drummer, but I reconsidered when I realized how sensitive and rashy he was, how he shrank away from other children and clung to my legs at the park, yet was shyly charismatic. "You can be the reclusive singer-songwriter with semi-confessional lyrics."

We began with the three essential rock vocal flourishes. "*Ow ow, doo doo, whoa whoa,*" I said. "That's our first lesson."

"Whoa whoa" was easy enough. I'd already taught him to identify adult women who were not "mama" with the help of "She's a Lady."

"Whoa, whoa, whoa lady!" he'd sing when a jogger passed by. *Whoa, whoa, whoa lady* indeed. The essence of rock, distilled into four words, three of which were the same word. Perfect.

Then it was on to The White Stripes.

"The hardest button to button!" I sang. I pointed. "Now you!"

"Ow ow," he whispered, smiling shyly.

"It's pain! Belt it!"

"Ow ow," he giggled.

Next was the rock 'n' roll count-off. First we had to learn to count to four.

"One and two!" he'd yell.

"How about 'One, two, three, four!'"

"One and two and two!"

"What comes after two?"

"One!"

"Okay, we'll work on it. Then you can experiment with funny rhythms and stuff." I was imagining Thom Yorke at the beginning of "Polyethylene."

A coffeehouse in town began hosting free kids' music on Sunday mornings. Avid supporters of local musicians, we'd drag ourselves out of bed, get dressed, and schlep across town for the occasion. We sampled what felt like dozens of artists—not for nothing does the Chamber of Commerce proclaim Austin "The Live Music Capital of the World"—but in retrospect was only four.

The first time, we heard the mellow musical stylings of Colonel Josh, who accompanies himself on six-string while he sings about the "toothbrush train" and putting your toys and books away so you'll be able to find them later. Colonel Josh is formerly of the bluegrass-hybrid performance collective The Asylum Street Spankers, whose songs I had to retire from rotation at home because they're all about grass and ass ("Shave 'Em Dry," "Funny Cigarette"). What better compromise than a kid-themed Spanking?

Though Colonel Josh was really likable, something was missing: He didn't *rock*. Neither did the first album by The Jelly Dots. Music teacher Doug Snyder formed The Jelly Dots in collaboration with his peewee guitar students and recorded them on an adorable CD entitled *Music Is Cool*. The songs are about cookies and cats named Ralph. They are delicate and reminiscent of Elliott Smith—minimalistic, angular indie pop. This was good—I liked it a lot—but I wasn't sure if my toddler would dance to it. There were no splash cymbals.

One morning we walked in the door of our coffeehouse to find two grown men in orange utility jumpsuits and hard hats operating crude puppets and singing about teeth.

I stopped in my tracks. "Okay, I need coffee. Immediately."

"Are you seeing that too?" Jim asked.

"Yes."

Our friend Moz the Wonder Baby and his parents were there. Moz's dad, Bruce, went apeshit for these guys. "It's the coolest thing ever! It's Tenacious D for kids!" he cried. (I'm not entirely sure that regular Tenacious D isn't for kids, aside maybe from the f-bombs.) "I think these guys have to do this as part of their community service," he concluded.

"Do y'all ever think about doing a kids' show here?" I asked him. Bruce plays and sings in a bluegrass band called The Boxcar Preachers.

He thought for a while. "Hadn't even occurred to me," he admitted. Their songs are about shallow gravesites, heroin addiction, and microsurgical vasectomy reversal.

Meanwhile, several of the toddlers were inspired to spin furiously to the music like Sufis, while Baldo sat riveted to my lap in a state of sensory-overload catatonia. He neither moved nor spoke for the entirety of their twenty-minute set. He didn't even touch his *horchata*.

The troubadours onstage called themselves The Telephone Company. Naturally, they had CDs for sale.

"We have to get one." I prodded Jim toward the stage. "No one will believe this actually happened. We'll have proof."

He engaged in conversation with one of the guys for about ten minutes, while Baldo pinned me to the chair and the other toddlers rushed the stage. He came back empty-handed.

"The kids took all the CDs. Their parents paid for them afterward."

"Damn!"

"But the guy is really cool. His name is Chef."

"Chef?"

"Well, okay, his name's actually Jason, but he goes by Chef."

"Is he a chef?"

"No."

"Oh." Kids' music is *fakakta*.

The Telephone Company doesn't bother with didactic songs about why it's important to put your books and toys away, from which I gathered that they were not themselves parents. Uncles, maybe. Given to strange flights of fancy about mustaches who run away and teeth who get married. Musically it's very Dada, with repetitive, jangly guitar chords and call-and-response character vocals with weird mic effects. It's the kind of thing your ironic hipster friends give your kid for his birthday (along with maybe a vintage Japanese wind-up robot toy with small swallowable parts and lead paint) and you put it on the very back of a tall shelf and forget about it until after bedtime months from now, when you're inebriated in the living room and you put it on because it's funny, except after you listen to a couple of tracks, you get completely paranoid because teeth aren't supposed to get married. So then you call your friend because you need someone to talk you down, and the friend says, "So was that not a good gift?" and you can't answer because your teeth will run away and elope if you open your mouth.

Another show, by a group called Nommi, promised "radical music for kids." That was cool, I guess, but I needed more information. Radical like The Clash? Radical like Billy Bragg? Radical like a hippie singing a neverending, dirge-like protest song at the Capitol rotunda? What were we dealing with here? Rhymes and toy piano protesting the WTO? Would there be tooth puppets? I wasn't sure I could deal with puppets.

Nommi was Spinal Tap minus the puppet show. Their amps went up to eleven. They had a full drum set and electric bass. They even had a sweaty guy in a Hawaiian shirt bashing a tambourine. Their singer ran around the stage like Wayne Famous while he sang about physical fitness. I waited for maternity bras to be unhooked and flung onstage. My son curled up in my lap and nursed constantly for reassurance, while the toddler audience surged around us like a tsunami.

"It's Baby Altamont!" I cried to Jim.

"What?" he yelled.

"I want The Telephone Company to come back," Bruce opined.

"I'm going to ask them to turn it down," his wife added.

At last I understood why kids' music didn't rock: because any bar-band yahoo can sing "The Wheels on the Bus" and work a roomful of toddlers into a lather, especially if cookies and *horchata* are for sale nearby. They freak out and crash in the car afterward, still dizzy from spinning. That's not necessarily a bad thing. It's fun to be goofy and run on fructose sometimes.

But what I really wanted to share with my son was *sincerity*. Music with a feeling behind it, something authentic and palpable. You know Ice-T means it when he says we shouldn't sell out, we should just yell out. You know Grover means it when he says that he is big and tall and very smart and kind of cute and wonderful.

I don't want a chokeload of whimsy shoved in my face; I could do without the slide whistles and toddlers in singsong unison. There has to be a balance. We need to have fun together; we can have handclaps and pop hooks, and we can sing about hot dogs and holes in the sea because these things are fun. It doesn't have to rock. It doesn't have to be cool. But it's got to be real.

THE INEVITABLE REMARKS
ABOUT ANDREA YATES

I DON'T GET IT, she wote. *Can postpartum depression really make a woman kill?*

We were discussing—as was just about everyone at the time—Andrea Pia Yates, the suburban Houston housewife who killed her five children in the summer of 2001 by drowning them in the bathtub.

How could a mother do that? the woman wanted to know.

We were talking on an Internet message board for mothers in Austin, but we weren't really communicating. A couple of people had already tried to explain. Postpartum depression is not postpartum *psychosis.* There's been some psychiatric mismanagement, some misuse of Haldol, someone alleged.

Okay, the woman said. *But I still don't understand.*

Then came the inevitable follow-up: *Is postpartum depression real?*

I sighed.

I'd stumbled into the forum looking for answers of my own. When you are home with a baby and you are depressed, your options for outreach are limited. You are not flitting around the coffee shop with a happy baby in a travel system. You are probably not wearing any pants. You may have fifteen minutes of fitful napping before the baby is screaming again.

Here was a forum online, one with a section devoted to discussion of PPD, ostensibly among mothers who are dealing with it, who are fighting it. I was looking for another depressed mother anywhere I could find her. Yet the only post was from a doubter, a "good" mother who said, *But I never felt that way. How could she?*

Wherever you go, you will find people who don't believe in postpartum depression. For whatever reason. It's an urban legend. It's like the Twinkie Defense; it was invented by "feminists" to apologize for filicide. Meanwhile, you're sitting there with it.

Until those of us who battle it and win—or at least cope—speak up, parental depression will enter public discourse only when the unthinkable happens. When a person loses her mind entirely. When reality slips away from her and she believes that, as surely as these words are printed on a page, something evil has possessed her family and must be banished with extreme measures. When she has become psychotic. When she has tried to kill herself twice in the span of a month and failed. When she has been hospitalized repeatedly. When she has accrued literally thousands of pages in her medical record. When she has refused to take the medication prescribed for her after her first suicide attempt and has begun mutilating her own body. When she has stopped feeding her children. When she has become convinced that hidden cameras in the ceiling of her home—at this point a 350-square-foot bus converted into a trailer house by her husband—are spying on her and the television is speaking to her. When she has finally entered a catatonic state for ten days.

This was Andrea Yates on July 20, 1999, long before any of us began to talk about her problems. Shortly thereafter, her husband, Rusty, moved the family to Clear Lake, a suburb far away from Andrea's psychiatrist. Her new physician, Dr. Mohammed Saeed, discontinued her medication, the antipsychotic Haldol, and urged her to "think positive thoughts"—a challenge for someone so debilitated that she had recently stopped talking altogether.

Two days after Saeed released her from an inpatient hospital stay with this advice, she systematically killed all her children and laid their bodies in the family bed. One child still clutched strands of Andrea's hair, yanked out in a struggle.

Andrea told a prison psychiatrist, "My children weren't righteous. They stumbled because I was evil. The way I was raising them, they could never be saved. They were doomed to perish in the fires of hell."

Her words echoed the teachings of Michael Woroniecki, an unordained minister who preached that "bad mothers who are going to hell create bad children who will go to hell." Woroniecki began his career evangelizing on the streets of Grand Rapids, Michigan, but was essentially forced from town after he harangued a woman who was trying to buy tickets for a circus. He was charged with disorderly conduct. He moved on to spread his message elsewhere, such as the campus of Brigham Young University, where Woroniecki called students "Mormon scumbags" and handed out self-authored pamphlets entitled "The Witch and the Wimp" with his wife and six children.

"As man was created to dominate, God reveals that woman was

created to be his helpmeet," Woroniecki wrote. "Thus the role of woman is derived, not from culture, but from the sin of Eve at the creation of the world."

It was at one of these demonstrations—at Auburn University in the mid-1980s—that Michael Woroniecki met Rusty Yates. Subsequently, Andrea became passionately devoted to Woroniecki's teachings.

Like most of Woroniecki's followers, Andrea corresponded with the traveling minister by mail. A dedicated search on the Internet unearths videos of Woroniecki's teachings—long-distance instructions for his flock, some posted by disgruntled students who've since rejected their leader. Before a plain backdrop, he speaks at length of the need to raise children righteously, lest they face the fires of hell. And I do mean that literally. Woroniecki describes the only godly mother: "a submitted woman who's got the fear of God in her heart for what her mother Eve has done." In a chilling moment he urges, "Whoever causes one of these little ones who believe in me to stumble, it is better for him that a heavy millstone be hung around [the child's] neck and he be drowned in the depths of the sea."

Perhaps we can begin to answer the question: *How could a mother do that?*

Yet it isn't only mothers who kill seemingly without warning. Consider Delfin Bartolome, by all reports a mild-mannered, fifty-five-year-old father of three. After picking up his twenty-seven-year-old autistic son from a nearby school for adults with developmental disabilities, Bartolome shot him twice in the chest and put the .357-caliber handgun to his head.

"I can understand where that man had gotten to," Mary Kate Saunders, another parent of an autistic child, told *The Orange County Register.* "You just pray you never get there."

Parents of autistic children are famously desperate, due to the extreme *lifelong* pressures in raising their children. Danielle Blais of Montreal drowned her six-year-old son, Charles-Antoine, in the bathtub in 1996. Carmen Lahaie, the president of the Autism Society of Greater Montreal, told *The Toronto Globe and Mail,* "Ms. Blais's act was unacceptable but understandable."

Janine Albury-Thomson of New Zealand strangled her daughter, Casey, in 1998.

Daniela Dawes of Sydney, Australia, was being treated for depression when she suffocated her ten-year-old son, Jason, and then attempted unsuccessfully to kill herself.

How could these parents do that?

In an article about the Bartolome murder-suicide, Jon Shestack, another parent to a child with autism, told *The Orange County Register,* "I don't look at (the murder-suicide) and think that guy was an alien or a monster. I just think how terribly sad and hopeless he might have felt. I can imagine it, because I can understand the burden on families."

When parents feel hopeless—when there is no respite care available, when their children's needs exceed their own compassion, when they have become depressed or psychotic, when there is no other way out but death—they are capable of murder.

None of this is to suggest that murder is excusable. It is not, and to suggest otherwise devalues the lives of the victims. Yet it is also not *inexplicable*. There are reasons for these tragedies, and it is incumbent upon all parents to understand them. To the poster on that message board: Yes, it is real. It is possible to love your children and kill them with your own hands. It is sad and horrific and wrong, but it is possible.

In writing this chapter, I was literally unable to keep up with reports of filicide. On November 22, 2004, a month before my deadline, Dena Schlosser of Dallas cut the arms off her daughter, Margaret, almost a year old. Margaret Schlosser bled nearly to death in her crib and expired at the hospital shortly after her mother was apprehended. Dena Schlosser still held a knife in her hand when police arrived.

I was revising this chapter on December 3, when Andrea Labbe of Toronto stabbed her husband, two of their three young daughters, and finally herself. At the time of this writing, police have refused to comment upon speculations that Labbe was suffering from postpartum psychosis or a report (broken in *The Toronto Sun*) that Labbe left a suicide note.

These cases inspire a frenzy of finger-pointing: Who was asleep at the switch when these women decided to kill their children? The Ontario Women's Health Network cited the Labbe case in its argument against proposed cuts in funding for hospital-based postpartum support services. The Schlosser family, on the other hand, had been investigated by Child Protective Services months before Margaret's murder, when Dena ran out of the house screaming, leaving her children behind. (Her five-year-old daughter chased her on a bicycle.) Though the incident suggests a possible psychotic episode, the basis for the investigation was child neglect. In any event, Dena Schlosser was judged mentally fit six months before she fatally mutilated her infant daughter.

Others point to cultural factors surrounding the killings. Like Andrea Yates, Dena Schlosser was profoundly influenced by a fundamentalist minister who preaches that women are innately wicked, redeemed only through submission to their husbands. Doyle Davidson, of Water of Life Ministries, had, in fact, been arrested after trying to "cast the devil" out of a rebellious female parishioner. Dena's stepfather, a licensed therapist, told the Associated Press, "This diminishing of women, this diminishing of women's powers, women's importance, referring to women as jezebels, I think, further undermines an already fragile ego state that Dena's experiencing."

"I'm an apostle and I'm a prophet," Davidson countered. "I only teach what's in the Bible and that's what makes them mad."

Michael Woroniecki likewise denies that his teachings played a role in Andrea Yates's psychosis. "I'm responsible for what I preach," he told the newspaper *Central Michigan Life*. "I can't be responsible for what they do with it."

Woroniecki blames Rusty for the deaths. "[Andrea] was a very caring, loving, intelligent woman. When [she] was put in that kind of pressure cooker, it was too much for her. [Rusty] let Andrea get into that situation, where she needed help. Then, he couldn't help her and wouldn't recognize that she needed him and Jesus. He let Andrea suffer under that."

TIME reporter Michelle McCalope quoted Rusty Yates in eulogizing his five children: "Andrea asked me about kids. She said 'do you want boys or girls?' I said I wanted to get a basketball team first, then we can talk about girls."

Yet Yates's brother and mother told *Good Morning America* that Rusty had never changed a diaper.

Eventually I began to find certain answers of my own.

I met a mother online whose PPD had verged on psychosis. She wrote to me in a private message: *I don't tell many people this, but I am telling you because I know how you feel. I got to a point that I was afraid to be left alone with [my son]. I understood how those women killed their children.* She was beginning to lose touch with reality. Driving back from the library, she sat at a stop sign a mile from her house, completely unsure in which direction to turn.

Another wrote to me: *This is the ultimate uncensored truth that I rarely admit to anyone. For the first two to three years of his life I truly disliked my son. He had colic and reflux and asthma and I was convinced he was autistic (he is not). He hated to be held and would fight me—he threw things and hit me all the time. He didn't nap, he didn't sleep at night. I tried co-sleeping, I tried letting him scream, I tried all the methods, I took him to strange doctors. He turned two in June of 1999, and that summer was the worst summer of my life. I felt like my soul was dead, and frankly, I was pissed [because it was my son's] fault.*

That fall, she returned to full-time paid work outside the home. ("It was the only way I could ever survive.") To everyone's surprise, the child flourished in Montessori preschool. Now, she says, "He's the kind of kid everyone loves. Strangers think he's great. He's always the teachers' favorite and of course no one believes he wasn't a cuddly, happy, Gerber baby."

Why do some of us survive while others slip away—into profoundly delusional thinking, into sudden, appalling violence against the very people we love? That's really the question the other mother was asking us online. What separates you—monstrous and perverse, a Medea—from me? Where is the line between a mother with "normal" problems germane to her station—the fatigue, the loneliness, the isolation, the worry, the constant interruption of her thoughts and actions—and a mother who snaps?

Until you've actually felt your brain slip out from under you, your answers to this question will be purely theoretical. Until you've actually had unwished-for thoughts in your head, thoughts you couldn't shake away, thoughts that didn't fade, thoughts that lingered so long they turned you upside down and became real. Until they replaced you and you were no longer there. Maybe you even felt yourself dissolving, like sugar. It's the strangest sensation I've ever had, to feel my personality separate into its component parts and very nearly disintegrate while my body remained entire. I could walk around my apartment touching things, but someone else perceived the sensations.

Once you have been there, you know where the line is.

When I was pregnant, I became convinced that I was going to abuse my child sexually. The idea just popped, fully formed, into my mind one day, apropos of evidently nothing. At twenty-nine years old, I did not have an abuse history, either as a victim or a perpetrator. *Why*, I wondered, *am I thinking this?* I had read nothing recently about sexual abuse. I'd been buried in my work as an editor. I was reading a textbook about human nutrition. It was dry and technical, suggestive of nothing beyond peptide strings. I hardly watched the news. I knew abuse survivors, but we weren't actively discussing the problem at the moment, and I had always been a sympathetic and properly horrified listener. There was no reason that I should suddenly become obsessed with pedophilia.

The thoughts bombarded me. Eventually I would spend all day struggling to squeeze them out. I could focus on nothing else. I'd sit glazed-eyed through meetings I was supposed to lead. I'd mumble my way through conversations with the people I knew. I'd sit for hours without speaking while battling myself inside. I'd drive seven or eight blocks out of the way to avoid a middle school on my way home from work. Kids ran track and practiced football outside at that time of day, and I was terrified of what I might think or feel, even though I had no reason to suspect myself of anything untoward. Several times a day, my composure would break and I would cry quietly, dreading what I would inevitably do to my child. I knew that, statistically speaking, women were less likely to commit sexual abuse of minors (the figure is about 14 percent). But what if I were an anomaly, a truly irregular person, like Karla Homolka, the submissive wife who helped her sociopathic husband sedate, rape, and kill her sister? I knew it was a long shot. But could I prove that I was normal? I couldn't.

I told no one of these thoughts, especially not my husband or my doctor. Indeed, writing these words is my first confession. I have written and erased it several times. I realize saying these words could have consequences for me and for my family. Yet I was, at that time, certain that despite my best intentions, I was going to abuse and corrupt my own child. It didn't matter if I wanted to or not, if I was ashamed or disgusted with myself; I'd do it anyway.

I can't explain why, but the feelings finally passed. I'd spent two weeks, easily, frantically trying to reassure myself that I was *not one of those people*. And in those two weeks I'd seen how easily a compulsive and irrational notion could take hold. How easily I could come to be a stranger to myself. How hard it was to fight the pull of insanity. Even now, I feel at times that an obsessive or depressive episode could happen in the next moment. But I feel it calmly, if you can imagine that. I can't prove to myself that my next thought won't be terrifying and unwanted, just as I can't prove to myself that my house will not be obliterated by a meteor, or that I won't have a heart attack as soon as I stand up. Since I can neither prove nor disprove any of these things, surely I can't remain captive to the possibility.

I do know that I could never harm my child. If I ever felt the temptation, I'd resist it at any cost. I'd kill myself if I had to. Yet I recognize that I sit here with advantages many other women do not have. I have not been brainwashed. I sought help and received it because within my personal history is the belief—the knowledge—that mental illness need not be kept secret, despite our collective fear of it. I have not been turned out of hospitals unwell, dominated by a loutish husband. I do not have three children under the age of three. But the significant difference between their lives and mine is that I never really went under. I just got close enough to the water to see my reflection.

MAMA'S NIGHT OUT

V. AND I ARE BARRELING DOWN Red River Street, listening to Samhain on the stereo. She's wearing a hot pink miniskirt and strappy black wedges that show off her ankle tats. Her pedicure is pink to match, and her hair, cut in a chunky, rocker-chick long bob, is streaked with platinum and fire-engine-red bitch streaks. She's powering up on an Odwalla Bar. We've got drinking on our minds.

Elmo watches from the back seat. We have to move aside the other maternal accoutrements when we pick up J.: some squeaky books, the ruffly pink dress from V.'s daughter's first birthday, resurrected for a photo shoot at Picture People. J. has just bleached her Jean Seberg microcut white and is bouncing up and down in the wagon's back seat. Her husband, L., has been listening to our conversation at home in Katy; she's accidentally dialed her cell. The bars of Red River and Sixth Street blip past—Red Eyed Fly, Beerland, Club DeVille. We're going where Waylon's on the jukebox and the ladies' room is an old train car outfitted with toilets and double sinks.

M. and A. are already waiting: smokes out, glasses half full of whatever they ordered in the precarious minutes after the waitress came by. Lactating mothers choose hastily; everything has been off limits to us, so where do we begin? A greyhound? A sidecar? A beer?

A Bombay Gibson? A. has a Tequila Sunrise, M. its equivalent in vodka. It's whiskey sours for me. V. is our cheerful designated driver; she gets a Shirley Temple and Chex mix for dinner and doesn't seem to mind at all.

By the time the band comes on at nine, we've talked about polyamory, student loans, abusive partners, abortions, BDSM, Annie Sprinkle, Andrea Dworkin, *The Best of British Spanking, Volume 8*, military enlistment, marijuana, Judaism, divorce, LiveJournals. We've compared our SSRIs and our mothers. One of us reveals that she half-jokingly teases her spouse about infantilization, waggling the diaper covers at him and calling him "babypants." We used to date skinny, wan-faced Morrisey manqués but wound up married to big hairy bears, all of us. We have half-finished bachelor's degrees and half-finished packs of cloves gone stale. Between us there are two caesareans, two home births, three doulas, one induction, two cases of preeclampsia, one preemie, jaundice, two neonatal heart murmurs, Nubain, morphine. M.'s phone rings: The caller has had two home births attended by V.'s midwife; one birth involved a cervical lip. Meanwhile, older couples are two-stepping to the music, and a guy in a straw summer-weight cowboy hat asks J. to dance.

We peel out of the parking lot after midnight. Some of us have leaking breasts. We go the wrong way on Fifth ("I swear, I haven't been drinking," V. insists) and head back through downtown, past the bars and the clubs and the people milling about with their own secrets inside.

PLAYGROUP
DRINKING GAME

"THE PLAYGROUP":

> Two parts Knudsen Hibiscus Cooler
>
> One part inexpensive vodka
>
> One part Pedialyte, any flavor (any flavor, to prevent dehydration and extend play)
>
> Mix ingredients together in small sippy cup (pref. two-handled). Add ice cube and shake vigorously; serve.

Rules of Play:

Players who do not have a sippy cup available will automatically pick up a two-drink penalty and must consume their beverage from whatever receptacle is handy (e.g., sports bottle, Neti pot, oral syringe, dirty ashtray, athletic shoe).

If a grown-up uses the word "poopy," that person drinks.

If a child uses the word "poopy," everyone drinks.

All drink if a child asks to nurse (with or without words).

All drink if a child is learning how to use the potty (once for each child).

All drink if a child takes a toy from another child.

Finish your glass if your child is the thief.

All drink every time a child cries.

Finish your glass every time a mother or father cries.

All drink whenever a box of baby wipes is opened.

Drink twice whenever you eat a snack intended for a child (e.g., graham crackers, arrowroot cookies, zwieback toast).

All drink when the following topics are raised:

frequency of sexual relations

pornography/the sex industry

reliable automobiles

real estate (including neighborhood comparisons)

recipes

religion (including Wicca and earth-worship)

movies

cable-access television

hair color

job hunting

dogs/puppies

preschool

Drink twice if:

The recipes are vegan or wheat-free.

Recipes are actually exchanged.

Anyone has had sexual relations in the past forty-eight hours.

Anyone's car is in the shop.

A borrowed object is returned.

Finish your glass if:

Your child vomits or defecates explosively (sufficient to cause staining outside the diaper).

A child hits another child with an implement of any nature (e.g., shape-sorting cube, umbrella, machete).

WHEN YOU ARE
STRONG ENOUGH

WHEN YOU ARE STRONG ENOUGH, you will drink a cup of coffee *in toto*. It will still be hot when you finish it.

When you are strong enough, you will be able to sleep.

When you are strong enough, you will surprise yourself by singing absentmindedly out loud.

When you are strong enough, you will not even realize that you are driving on the Highway 183 flyover.

When you are strong enough, you will floss your teeth.

When you are strong enough, you will be able to offer help to someone with a problem, whatever its nature. Dead auto battery? Broken heart? Infestation of sugar-eating ants? You will remember that you have expertise in such matters, back in a corner of your head where your depression used to be.

When you are strong enough, you may develop a renewed interest in current events.

When you are strong enough, your love for your child will astound you.

When you are strong enough, food will taste a lot better. You will like burritos. Go ahead and have one.

When you are strong enough, you will be more able to have

civil, coherent conversations with the people you love.

When you are strong enough, you will be a better friend to yourself. It sounds really platitudinous but is true.

When you are strong enough, don't be surprised if you get angry. When you are strong enough, you will direct your anger where it belongs. When you are strong enough, you can start to fight back.

When you are strong enough, you can advocate for your child. When you are strong enough, you will be a major ass-kicking motherfucker.

When you are strong enough, you will rediscover your CD collection.

When you are strong enough, don't forget to write your thank-you notes. And I'm not talking about thanking Aunt Mildred for the duck-print baby kimono.

When you are strong enough, you will see the frustration in the faces of the parents around you. Reach out to them, even if they are strangers. Tell them they're doing a good job. Commiserate with them. So many times I fell apart in public places and was horrified and ashamed of how my baby cried and how poorly I coped. Nobody was brave enough to talk to me. When you meet a new mother, ask her how *she* is. Sincerely.

When you are strong enough, you will remember how your obsessive thoughts were like a machine that ran faster and faster, feeding on its own power, getting hotter and louder, glowing, exerting. You will remember how it felt to look in the mirror while you were brushing your teeth and stare at parts of your face as if you'd never seen them before. You will remember how it felt to dig at yourself, to cut yourself with whatever you used, to drink whatever you drank, to swallow whatever you took. You will never forget what it felt like. You will always feel one step away from falling backward into it.

This information will become a part of who you are, permanently. Keep it. Now that you are a parent, you will need it. You will hold on to it while you watch your child struggling through life. It will not be easy. You will have bigger problems than exploded diapers and teething, though those were your first lessons. You held on tightly to a person in pain, knowing you couldn't cure him. You couldn't help him. You were confused and scared, but you held on anyway because that person needed you to. Maybe it would make a difference that you were there, that you were holding on, that you would not let go, that you would do anything, that you would never give up, even if the pain never stopped. You would hold on forever if you had to.

You'll do it again. You're going to have to explain how people can suffer. You're going to have to explain what a lie is. You're going to have to explain how there are some things a person can never have, can never do. Now that you have held a baby and walked the floor for hours at a time, you can begin to hold on to someone who has just learned the meaning of death. Now that you have squirted medication into a screaming, toothless mouth, you can begin to hold on to someone who has become an addict. Now that you have kept yourself together when your own brain threatened to blow you apart, you can begin to hold on to someone who is depressed. Now that you have kept yourself alive, you can begin to hold on to someone who wants to die. And just as with baby Zantac and colic cures, there's no guarantee that it will work. But you will do what you can. You will do everything you can.

Congratulations.

THE TODDLER TRAVELS

Friday

I am writing this sentence on a swaggy notepad from a National Hotel Chain, room 1036. We are 1,500 miles from home with a seventeen-month-old who has, since our departure two days ago, cut four molars and an incisor. We have all been awake since 4:30 AM. This is Extreme Parenting.

We are here with approximately three hundred mamas, daddies, babies, and kids at an event called Mama Gathering 2003. We are talking with one another about educational options, "peaceful parenting," the mass media, teen parenting, zine publishing. One session, open only to adult women, is devoted to empowerment through stripping; another elucidates the world of sex toys. There are dreadlocked hippies in hemp drawstring pants; there are hip-hugging scenester chicks with little cat's-eye glasses; there are Radical Cheerleaders in jackboots and split skirts. There are toddlers wearing marabou and Elton John sunglasses. Then there is a guy named Bruce whose t-shirt proclaims, in 1970s felt iron-on letters, SPERM DONOR DAD; he spends the session picking his toenails and hyping his zine about taking preschoolers to political demonstrations. Others in the group are bona fide Internet celebrities.

I initially react with a crisis of coolness. I am not worthy of these people. The Crib Police are going to break down our door and put the baby back in our bed. They'll confiscate our crappy processed snacks and make us unschool. Moreover, all the other mothers are bonding at the bar, emitting girlish squeals and puffs of secondhand smoke. I feel a sniftit coming on. Sure enough, it turns out that I am starting my second postpartum period. Unprepared, I stuff a size 4 diaper in my pants and head to Ralph's.

None of the hotel's other guests know what to do with us—not the New-Agey, spiritual people using the ballroom, not the family reunioners wearing matching t-shirts, not the Korean tour group. If you really want to freak people out, assemble a large group of children and mothers in a public place without apparent purpose. That's some freaky shit—freakier than a Critical Mass bicycle demonstration or mimes in a park. People get scared. What are *they* doing here? Don't they have somewhere else to be?

We conclude the evening with a potluck at Chace Park. Toddlers run amok, climbing trees and rolling down hills. A single student mama is shooting her thesis film; her four-year-old feeds strawberries and a non-vegan chocolate cake to Baldo. There will be eczema tomorrow, but it's worth it.

I am beginning to feel comfortable with motherhood at last. My child is doing nothing other children aren't doing. Nobody has x-ray vision to see through my pants to my caesarean scar. I have something, at least one thing, in common with everyone here. I take a deep breath, the first in a long, long time.

Saturday
I miss the morning section on educational options because Baldo is teething, screaming, and worming around. We spend the ninety minutes climbing up and down the stairs, then passing out in our room.

The bad news is that lunch, for us, is sandwiches with hummus and sprouts. All the other available options have some form of nuts. Why do vegans eat so many nuts? Don't they worry about allergies? We are truly becoming The People Who Could Eat Nothing. (Later we will appreciate more fully the cross-sensitivity between nuts and chickpeas and tahini, which rules out even hummus.) The good news is that Jim volunteers to go shopping on Melrose with Baldo, leaving me to attend the last two sessions solo. I can hit the bar with other conventioneers—part of the Minneapolis contingent, the sound recordist from the thesis film, and a Los Angeles mama with a lip ring and Bettie Page hairdo. I have just enough time to pound a whiskey sour on my almost empty stomach and run off to my session on zines and alternative media, where I drunkenly accost the moderator.

Dinner is a party with a buffet. Sugared-up and napless toddlers surround the toy pile like carnivorous ants from the Amazon eyeballing a cricket corpse. Baldo patiently waits his turn for a kid-sized electric guitar with pickups and everything; then he begins pounding it into the floor. Jim takes it from his hands, but I can tell he is secretly pleased. "Like Kurt," he tells me later.

A crunchy couple in line with us for avocado burritos observes Baldo and asks how he's sleeping. Their four-month-old is slumped angelically on the father's shoulder. We explain about the teething. I gush about how I don't want to use Tylenol—it's hard on their livers and can have adverse reactions, and I know I really should be able to just use organic chamomile tea or clove oil and nurse on demand. I should be supporting our cooperative supermarket. I'm getting really wound up, and they're waving their hands at me to calm me down. "I'd totally do it," the woman says. And the Baby Orajel? "Oh, yeah," she agrees. "If I had to, sure."

Sunday

After the gathering ends, we find a park to play in. Baldo chases ducks. Despite the heat, families are out in force, barbecuing. Police cruisers are skimming the parking lot—this being L.A., and so many of the families being non-Caucasian—but they find nothing objectionable in the bouncy castles and Frisbee dogs.

As we pack up, I notice that Baldo has skinned a knee. Blood is dried on his shin. He never made a peep about it, and I clean it with water from my germy sport bottle. It will be healed and invisible within a week.

Infancy is officially over.

Monday

We have errands to run in L.A., including a visit to the Directors' Guild of America building, where Jim has a meeting. Maybe I should be uncomfortable about our whole family barging in, but the office appears to be staffed entirely by women, and they know we're on vacation.

I breastfeed looking out the window at the Sunset Strip. As we are trooping down the hall, people come out of their offices to see the baby. I'm afraid we're disturbing them, but they're smiling and laughing, telling Baldo he's cute, which makes him preen.

Tuesday

Morning is spent at the beach. We heft Baldo's stroller and carry it like an imperial litter onto the sand. He's never been to the ocean before, but he toddles into it fearlessly, laughing.

He only cries when we eventually have to pack up and clean off. We hold him under the showers and rinse the sand off. The water is cold, and he curls up like a fish.

Wednesday and Thursday

It is raining for the second day, forcing us to scrap our outdoor plans.

I tire out at the aquarium. I want to sit down and stop making decisions for a while—where to go, when to leave, where to park, what to eat, whom to call. I want to make a sandwich and sit on my own couch.

The fantasies of being single intrude. If somebody gets hurt and needs a Band-Aid, all heads turn toward me. I'm The Mom now. I'm the one who brings along home remedies for heartburn, jellyfish stings, road rash. I'm the end of the line.

I slump on a bench. Jim takes Baldo outside to see the hands-on stuff. Other tourists are slouching around stupidly—going in the exits, standing in the middle of doorways. I feel contempt for us all.

We overfish and dump waste. We spread *Caulerpa taxifolia* every-where. I couldn't even look at the guitar-nosed shovelfish without wanting to eat it.

Jim's red cap bobs toward me. Baldo is grinning.

"We looked at all the animals," Jim reports. "And we touched the back of the swordfish and felt it move."

It's affirming when your child touches something for the first time. The neurons fire, and information becomes a sensation, then a memory, maybe even part of a personality. Maybe you've watched a person change forever. Maybe it's nothing. Maybe it's everything. It's not the "Maybe he'll be a brilliant biologist!" bit. Maybe he'll be a telephone lineman, but he'll be a telephone lineman who felt a swordfish react to his touch, who felt its scales ripple and smiled because it was beautiful.

Friday

Jim's family comes over to meet Baldo, many for the first time. Jim's "Aunt" Catherine is telling me about her daughter's colic.

"We'd all put on our pajamas at night and drive thirty miles until she stopped screaming," she explains. "If it hadn't been for my mother helping us, I don't know if we would have made it."

Then what? I want to ask. What does it mean to not make it? What would you have done?

I imagine that I am standing across from a thirty-years-older version of myself. She is holding a drink gracefully and laughing. She has become What We Mean When We Talk About Mothers: nurturing, encouraging, gentle, composed.

But she's still me. She finished her Tom Collins a little too quickly. She has a tiny little pinprick scar where her nostril used to be pierced.

And maybe when the party is over, when fiancées have been met and graduations celebrated and houses warmed, she will say her goodbyes and clack down the driveway, her keys in her pocket and Public Enemy waiting in the stereo.

AFTERWORD

YESTERDAY I HAD A MISERABLE DAY. Barely coping. I discovered a dead squirrel facedown in our grass and had to hustle Baldo inside. He broke out with a rash from grapes and cried through his nap. I syringed antihistamine into his mouth. I shoveled the squirrel into the trash and smoked a cigarette on the back porch—a bad habit I gave up while pregnant and that's returning gradually. I struggled to work on my book, burning up two precious hours after bedtime on a single paragraph.

It was a bad day. But it was one day.

On another day, a good day, we took Baldo to his first rock show—a kid-friendly band at a kid-friendly venue. The songs were about cookies and cats. I sat in a folding chair and watched my son inch away from me, taking hesitant steps into the world.

"I want to dance," he explained. But he didn't leave my side for long.

The band, friends of friends, performed "Race Cars Go" a second time, upon request from a kid in the balcony celebrating his seventh birthday. Then they did a song I remembered well from the first day of my pregnancy, when I sat in the living room listening to Elliott Smith.

I saw you in a perfect place
It's gonna happen soon but not today
So go to sleep and make the change
I'll meet you here tomorrow
Independence day
Independence day
Independence day

All the way home, Baldo sang the song's refrain: *Everybody knows, everybody knows.*

Everybody knows you only live a day, but it's brilliant anyway.

From such pain comes a beautiful idea, the kind you seize, and you chant the words like a catechism during nights that are long and sleepless and tearful. You chant them when you are desperate and miserable. You will be desperate and miserable. You will always be desperate and miserable.

But when you and your child learn to put words to a feeling, you can share it. There is power in speaking it. The first time you converse with your child, it's like every first date you've ever had all at once. *Do you like oranges? Should we wear the red shirt? Are you angry? You can say, "I am angry!"* At last, you will come to know your child as a person.

"I like Johnny Cash," my son told me one morning. Soon our bedtime and naptime stories were filled with his exploits. Johnny Cash went to Sears to buy a new hammer because he wanted to hang sheetrock in his bathroom. Johnny Cash rode the bus and went to the zoo. It was as if the Man in Black had reached down from the great beyond and thrown me a life preserver. In my dreams I sat beside him on a bench, thanking him.

My son prefers a certain shirt of mine, a vintage sleeveless smock with a strawberry print and a tiny lace collar. I wear it when I feel ironic and retro. When I see him in the morning on these days, his face broadens into the shy smile of the introverted child.

"I like these strawberries," he whispers.

I live in the moments when he registers something that pleases him. These moments are a minority in the world of a toddler. He is aggrieved by his pants, by a diaper, by big-kid underpants, by bath water, by his car seat. "My pants don't like me!" he cries. "The cottage cheese doesn't love me!" After twenty such incidents in a single morning, I am ready to deposit him in the arms of a kindly stranger and retire to the desert climes of Terlingua, Texas, where I will live out my days in blessed solitude, beating rattlesnakes from the door of my Airstream with a cane I have whittled of mesquite.

I do feel that way. Every mother feels that way. When my mother was an Air Force wife stationed in Turkey with my father, she'd threaten to run away with a camel caravan. However, she and I are not insane. We are overworked, aggravated, at wit's end. But we are not depressed. Now I can recognize the difference.

I keenly recall the days when the urge to self-destruct overwhelmed me. I remember how the urge to die was implacable; I'd hurt myself just to break the cycle of the death wish, to give myself a feeling with clear cause and effect, beginning and ending.

I have been depressed before. I will probably become depressed again. I can't live my life waiting for the other shoe to drop. It will or it won't.

More likely, I'll remain on the slippery slope of motherhood—frustration, depletion, exhaustion, boredom—between sanity and madness. We all live here. In so many moments I've wondered why we even make reference to "postpartum depression" when life with young children is so self-evidently crazy-making. Love is not enough to keep you happy. Why do we tell mothers this lie?

I recently addressed a group of mothers, speaking on the topic of motherhood and sanity. Their stories were legion: abusive partners, single motherhood and poverty, obsessive-compulsive and panic disorders, rivalrous siblings, children on the autism spectrum. One was married to a soldier in Iraq. Another had left an abusive man and run right into the arms of a therapist who mismedicated her, told her things would get better at home if she just accepted the situation. Another had a child screamier than mine and was trying to get by on what remains of welfare. These women are not experiencing postpartum depression as we (incorrectly) understand it, which is to say as a heartbreaking twist of hormones. They are experiencing postpartum *oppression*—the grind of getting by in a culture that systematically devalues women and their mothering, a culture that tells us not to ask for assistance, a culture that makes us jump through bureaucratic hoops to get the proper education and treatment for our special-needs children, a culture of doctors and "experts" and partners and friends and politicians who tell us we are to blame for everything we experience. For support, these mothers rely on the kindness of others: in-laws who might criticize their choices and insult them, friends who are intermittently available, partners who don't listen or don't care. This, too, is the slippery slope of motherhood. Too many of us are falling off, and we need to catch each other.

There are times when it is personally necessary to wave the flag of "postpartum depression." There are times when you might recognize that you have lost the ability to experience anything but rage and defeat. Your body can't sleep. Your mind won't stop racing. You can't breathe through the panic you feel. You are furious at yourself. You are hurting. You have become your shadow-self. Because "postpartum depression" exists, you can attach a name to your feelings and advocate for your needs or the needs of your partner or loved ones. You will improve your chances of being taken seriously if you can attach yourself to a psychological phenomenon agreed upon as legitimate by the medical firmament. You can access whatever resources you do have. You can restore yourself gradually. You can finally resume functioning as a human being. You have to do this first.

This is not to say that you will ever be "all better," or that your life will return to normal. It can't and shouldn't. Later on you must turn and help other mothers out of the swamp. Now you can begin chipping away at the lie that "good" mothers are happy, and that any deviation from the perceived notion of maternal bliss is abnormal or even pathological. For reasons I can't as yet explain, too many of us unconsciously subscribe to the Victorian ideal of the "angel in the house": the equanimitous and selfless caregiver who creates, at home, a sanctuary apart from the outside world—the pressures of her husband's occupation (for of course the "angel" is married to a male breadwinner), the corruptive influences of mass culture and social problems—and who educates and nurtures her children in a kind of protective Lucite sleeve. Our lives simply do not measure up, and we will make ourselves crazy trying. It is up to each of us to tell her story by talking to other parents, to men and women, to our elders who may have forgotten or deliberately disremembered the struggle to keep their heads above water while raising young children. Write about your experience or make art from it or stand in the middle of Babies "R" Us screaming about it. When someone asks you how you are, tell her or him the truth. Tell them you're having a fucking awful time of it if, in fact, you are. Tell them you are ambivalent. Tell them it's complicated. Tell them you're happy, but you have some regrets.

Approach another parent of small children—at the mall or the supermarket or a bus stop or wherever you happen to be—and show her or him kindness, regardless of whether the baby is in disposable diapers or nursing at the breast or eating a sugar cookie or wearing a $50 organic romper. Don't worry that you'll say something condescending or tin eared; you can apologize if you do. It is important for us to begin the conversation somewhere. Particularly, you must approach mothers who are unlike yourself—if indeed any two mothers are really truly unlike—and acknowledge the valiance of these women. I've seen serene, Earth-goddess, homeschooling midwives—the kind of mothers to whom I inevitably feel inferior because I'm a cigarette-smoking, coffee-swilling, meat-eating, Paxil-popping, sarcastic Texan loudmouth—break down before me and weep from the stress of trying to seem "together" all the time. (I suppose they don't have to worry about impressing me.) I've seen young mothers catch shit for being too young, older mothers catch shit for being too old. We catch shit for working outside the home and "abandoning" our children to paid care; we catch shit for leeching off society and partners who work if we do not. We catch shit if our children's skin isn't precisely the same color as ours. We catch shit if we leave a destructive marriage; we catch shit if we remain. If we love women, we catch shit from other mothers for being lesbian while we catch shit from other lesbians for being mothers. Nobody wins at this game.

Mothers of the world, we've got to have each other's backs. Without working together, we literally cannot survive. Because we are divided—into "working" and "stay-at-home" parents, into "natural" or "attachment" parents and "mainstream" parents—we remain marginalized *as a group*. We just haven't noticed, because we're too busy shooting each other down, trying to glean little nuggets of self-satisfaction from an enterprise that is still considered less significant than paid work, that we are still expected to conduct without disturbing the sanctity of public places and public policy, that we must perform without marring our bodies or our minds or imposing on our families and partners. We haven't noticed the price we pay for our choices, whichever choices they are. And we haven't noticed that there are, in our communities, wherever they are, tired and frantic parents who are circling the neighborhood in desperate tears with strollers or car seats and cranky siblings in tow. Your mission now is to find these people.

As for Baldo, Jim, and me: There is no conclusion to our story. We have put certain things behind us: our naturopath, teething remedies and tiny clothes, the baby sling—but the rest remains a part of our daily work. I flirt with tapering off my Paxil but haven't done it yet. Jim and I still argue about our responsibilities. We still apply a panoply of ointments to our son. I'm still nursing Baldo, who's still clingy and challenging as a toddler; I figure I ought to play to my strengths. It's still hard work, but I am better able to handle it. This is as close as human beings ever get to a sense of victory in our lives.

This past summer Jim had a vasectomy. In our own way, we grieved for the children we will not have. While Aunt Erin watched Baldo at home, I took Jim to the urologist (whose name—I kid you not—is Dick Chopp) and waited for an hour during the procedure. In the room with me, there was a mother with a toddler and an infant. She looked exhausted, yet I envied her. I envied her children because they will have a sibling; Jim and I do not, and now Baldo won't, either. For a while I'd weep when I saw a woman snuggling a contented newborn. In time, I realized I was crying for the experience I did not have, an experience I will never have with a child of my own. I will never have a gentle home birth; I will never have an easy baby to love. I will never look into the eyes of a child and feel instant joy. I will only remember hallucinating in the operating room and half-sleeping upright with an aching scar. Yet I choose to embrace these memories as my own. They are my history as a mother. They do count.

Sometimes I worry about having worn my resentment for

motherhood on my sleeve, but ultimately I have to embrace that as my own experience as well. I do not worry that Baldo will grow up thinking of himself as "difficult" for me. I know too many grown-up "difficult" children who have gone on to lead remarkably well-adjusted lives, whose relationships with their own mothers are candid but teasing and affectionate. Such is my step-cousin, who is, at the time of this writing, a thirteen-year-old ball of fire. He still sleeps little. He still drives his mother crazy. He's still a magnet for trouble. And he is very loved, even if his mother declares she'd have stopped at one child if he'd been the first.

We have to accept our children as the people they are and acknowledge our own limitations. I do not believe children are well served by benevolent disinformation about the struggles we have raising them. We will care for them and guide them gently through life, but we must also recognize that they will face their own demons in time. We have the opportunity to teach them resilience by example. We will present ourselves to them as survivors. It will be the truth.

NOTES

1. "Postpartum Depression," National Women's Health Information Center (NWHIC) (accessed September 6, 2004), www.4woman.gov/faq/postpartum.htm#4.
2. "Education of Adoptive Parents," *The Encyclopedia of Adoption* (accessed September 6, 2004), http://encyclopedia.adoption.com/entry/education-of-adoptive-parents/122/1.html.
3. Goodman, J. H., "Postpartum Depression in Fathers," *The Journal of Advanced Nursing,* vol. 45 (2004): 26–35.
4. "Recognizing Postpartum Depression," National Mental Health Association (NMHA), www.nlm.nih.gov/cgi/medlineplus/leavemedplus.pl?theURL=httP%3A%2F%2Fwww.nmha.org%2Fchildren%2Fppd.pdf.
5. Kleiman, Karen, "Ask the Experts: Can men get the postpartum blues?" Babycenter.com, www.babycenter.com/expert/3870.html; Kleiman, Karen, "Information for Husbands and Other Family Members," The Postpartum Stress Center, www.postpartum.com/information_for_family.html; Misri, Shaila, MD, FRCP(C), "Postpartum Depression and Anxiety," Wellmother.com, www.wellmother.com/postpartum.htm.
6. Karen Kleiman and Valerie Raskin, *This Isn't What I Expected: Overcoming Postpartum Depression* (New York: Bantam, 1994).
7. Postpartum Resource Center of Texas, www.texaspostpartum.org/PPD.html.
8. "Recognizing Postpartum Depression," NMHA.
9. Consider the 2003 case of Deanna LaJune Laney, a working-class woman who beat two of her sons to death and critically injured a third, then called sheriff's deputies to calmly report the crime. Or Naomi Gaines, an African-American woman who dropped her two sons into the Mississippi River outside of St. Paul, Minnesota, then jumped into the water to kill herself. Or Khoua Her, a Laotian immigrant who killed her six children, then attempted to strangle herself. The names that are household words—such as Andrea Yates and Susan Smith—belong to white, middle-class women, college graduates.

10. Hagen, Edward H., "The Functions of Postpartum Depression," www .anth.ucsb.edu/projects/human/ppd.pdf.

11. Amankwaa, L., "Postpartum Depression, Culture and African-American Women," *Journal of Cultural Diversity* (Spring 2003): 23–29.

12. Amankwaa, L. C. C., "Enduring: A grounded theory investigation of postpartum depression among African-American women," (doctoral dissertation, Georgia State University, 2000), *Dissertation Abstracts International*, 60, 03B.

13. Johnson, R. & Crowley, J., "An Analysis of Stress Denial," in *Mental Health in Black America* (H. Neighbors & J. Jackson, London: Sage Publications, 1996), 62–76.

14. Cox J. L., "Childbirth As a Life Event: Sociocultural Aspects of Postnatal Depression," *Acta Psychiatrica Scandinavica*, (1988): 344, 75–83.

15. Nonacs, Ruta M., "Postpartum Depression," eMedicine.com (2004), www .emedicine.com/med/topic3408.htm.

16. Song, Sora, "Too Posh to Push? As more pregnant women schedule C-sections, doctors warn that the procedure is not risk-free," *Time* (April 19, 2004).

17. Sears, William, *The Baby Book* (Boston: Little, Brown & Co, 1993).

18. Marc Weissbluth, MD, *Healthy Sleep Habits, Healthy Child* (New York: Fawcett, 1999).

RESOURCES

Postpartum Depression

Depression After Delivery, Inc. (DAD)
www.depressionafterdelivery.com
A national nonprofit organization providing information and support referrals since 1985 to families affected by postpartum depression. Sadly, the national office closed its doors in 2004, so the information line (previously 800-944-4773) is no longer available, but all of the organization's literature is available online for those who have access to the Internet. The website also contains a clearinghouse for volunteers who provide phone support to callers in the United States. (The organization provides outreach in British Columbia through the Pacific Postpartum Support Society.) The organization has been active in agitating for the Melanie Stokes Postpartum Depression Research and Care Act (HR-846), named for a Chicago woman who committed suicide after developing postpartum psychosis.

Postpartum Support International (PSI)
www.postpartum.net
Jane Honikman, Founding Director
Sherri Majors, Office Manager
Postpartum Support International
927 N. Kellogg Avenue
Santa Barbara, CA 93111 USA
voice: (805) 967-7636

fax: (805) 967-0608

email: PSIOffice@earthlink.net

Sponsored by Indiana University of Pennsylvania, this organization offers various resources for families with PPD, including an online support group with scheduled real-time chats and a message board for family members. The organization also provides information about local support services in most U.S. states and various countries, including China, the United Kingdom, Australia, New Zealand, and South Africa. The site is affiliated with Karen Kleiman, author of the definitive self-help book on PPD, *This Isn't What I Expected: Overcoming Postpartum Depression.*

The Ruth Rhoden Craven Foundation, Inc. for Postpartum Depression Awareness

Helena Bradford, Chairman

1339 Outreach Lane

Mt. Pleasant, SC 29464 USA

voice: (843) 881-2047

email: buzerhel@aol.com

Helena Bradford founded this organization in honor of her daughter, Ruth Craven, who committed suicide after the birth of her first child in 1999. The group provides support and referrals in South Carolina, and the group welcomes email inquiries.

Melanie's Battle: The Hidden Plague of Postpartum Psychosis and Depression

www.melaniesbattle.org

Carol Blocker

voice: (312) 225-1310

A page maintained by Carol Blocker, mother of Melanie Stokes.

The Center for Postpartum Health
www.postpartumhealth.com
Diana Lynn Barnes, Psy.D., MFT
20700 Ventura Boulevard, Suite 203
Woodland Hills, CA 91364 USA
voice: (818) 887-131
fax: (818) 887-1312
email: dlbarnes@postpartumhealth.com
Marriage and family therapist Diana Lynn Barnes writes frequently on postpartum depression and psychosis for the popular media, and her center provides group counseling and service referrals at two locations in Southern California. Several articles are available online.

Postpartum Dads: Helping Families Overcome Postpartum Depression
www.postpartumdads.org
A subgroup of Postpartum Support International devoted to information for the male partners of women with PPD. Includes guidance on relationship issues, dealing with the legal system, and other topics.

The Online PPD Support Group
www.ppdsupportpage.com
Tonya Rosenberg, Administrator
email: tonya@ppdsupportpage.com
This helpful site includes downloadable brochures, articles, an email support list, and an online discussion forum.

Suicide Prevention

Centre for Suicide Prevention (Canada)
www.suicideinfo.ca
Suite 320, 1202 Centre Street S.E.
Calgary, AB T2G 5A5 CANADA
voice: (403) 245-3900
fax: (403) 245-0299
email: csp@suicideinfo.ca
Not a crisis intervention service but an exhaustive library of English-language materials on suicide prevention. Home of the Suicide Prevention Training Programs (SPTP), which educate caregivers around the world.

Suicide Prevention Action Network (SPAN USA)
www.spanusa.org
1025 Vermont Avenue, NW, Suite 1200
Washington, DC 20005 USA
voice: (202) 449-3600
fax: (202) 449-3601
email: info@spanusa.org
This outreach and advocacy organization maintains a thorough list of resources regarding suicide prevention, including support for survivors.

The Kristin Brooks Hope Center (KBHC) and National Hopeline Network
www.hopeline.com
voice: (703) 837 3364 or (800) SUICIDE
email: info@hopeline.com
An invaluable network of crisis centers throughout the United States. The website also provides referrals to centers in Great Brit-

ain, Singapore, and Canada. Named for Kristin Brooks Rossell, who killed herself in 1998 while suffering from postpartum depression.

Gastroesophageal Reflux Disease and Food Allergies

DrGreene.com
www.drgreene.com
My favorite "expert" pediatrician who balances traditional allopathic sensibilities with an awareness of alternative treatments. No hard-line parenting dogma, just sensitive and well-considered medical advice for families.

The Food Allergy and Anaphylaxis Network
www.foodallergy.org
11781 Lee Jackson Hwy., Suite 160
Fairfax, VA 22033–3309 USA
voice: (800) 929-4040
email: faan@foodallergy.org
An excellent clearinghouse of information (including recipes, product recalls, and current activism) for people with (and parents of people with) food allergies. Includes a storefront of products, such as children's books about food allergies (including the *Alexander, The Elephant Who Couldn't Eat Peanuts* series) and swanky carriers for your epinephrine injector.

Pediatric/Adolescent Gastroesophageal Reflux Association (PAGER)
Jan Burns
voice: (888) 887-7729
email: refluxmom2@earthlink.net
An organization offering support and information concerning

pediatric and adolescent reflux since 1992. Along with Allegheny General Hospital, Center for Genomic Sciences, PAGER is, at the time of this writing, conducting a study of hereditary factors present in reflux. The organization offers volunteer call-back and email services, the "Reflux Digest" informational newsletter, and a bulletin board for reflux parents.

"Gastroesophageal Reflux in Infants"
Children's Medical Center of the University of Virginia
Stephen M. Borowitz
www.healthsystem.virginia.edu/internet/pediatrics/patients/
Tutorials/reflux/home.cfm
A first-rate online tutorial about the causes of and treatments for reflux, using animation, layperson's language, and clear illustrations to explain the phenomenon to sleepless and frustrated parents.

Life on the Reflux Roller Coaster
by Roni MacLean and Jean McNeil
$16.95, ISBN: 1-4137-0833-1
Publish America, (301) 695-1707
A self-published volume by two reflux parents, with a foreword by pediatric allergy specialist Dr. Doris Rapp, MD

Breastfeeding a Baby with Reflux
www.users.qwest.net/~fsdebra1/
Debbie Frost, Administrator
email: breastfeedingreflux-subscribe@yahoogroups.com
A Yahoo! group providing peer-to-peer support for breastfeeding women whose children suffer from reflux.

Books

The Bitch in the House: 26 Women Tell the Truth About Sex, Solitude, Work, Motherhood, and Marriage. Cathi Hanauer, editor. Perennial, 2003.

Buchanan, Andrea J. *Mother Shock: Loving Every (Other) Minute of It.* Seal Press, 2003.

Cusk, Rachel. *A Life's Work: On Becoming a Mother.* Picador, 2003.

Douglas, Susan and Meredith Michaels. *The Mommy Myth: The Idealization of Motherhood and How It Has Undermined Women.* Free Press, 2004.

Gore, Ariel. *The Mother Trip: Hip Mama's Guide to Staying Sane in the Chaos of Motherhood.* Seal Press, 2000.

Kleiman, Karen R. *The Postpartum Husband.* Xlibris Corporation, 2001.

Kleiman, Karen R. and Valerie Raskin. *This Isn't What I Expected: Overcoming Postpartum Depression.* Bantam, 1994.

Koppelman, Amy. *A Mouthful of Air.* MacAdam/Cage, 2003.

Lamott, Anne. *Operating Instructions: A Journal of My Son's First Year* (reprint). Ballantine Books, 1994.

Lazarre, Jane. *The Mother Knot* (reprint). Duke University Press, 1997.

Maushart, Susan. *The Mask of Motherhood: How Becoming a Mother Changes Our Lives and Why We Never Talk About It.* Penguin Books, 2000.

Mothers Who Think: Tales of Real-Life Parenthood. Camille Peri and Kate Moses, editors. Washington Square Press, 2000.

Resnick, Susan Kushner. *Sleepless Days: One Woman's Journey through Postpartum Depression.* St. Martin's Press, 2001.

Rich, Adrienne. *Of Woman Born: Motherhood as Experience and Institution (reprint).* W. W. Norton, 1995.

ACKNOWLEDGMENTS

I OWE A DEBT OF GRATITUDE to so many people for their help and support. First among them are the mothers who shared their lives with me, formally and casually. I give thanks for every mother who reassured me or lent a sympathetic ear during my depression and recovery. I am blessed by the friendship, wisdom, and spark of the "rebel mamas"—you ladies know who you are. This book (and its author) would not exist without you.

To the parents in my life and community: to Audrey Centola, my first mama friend; to Tifanie Charboneau; to Bruce and Andrea Citrin-Gardner; to Brook Son and Ken Green; to Christiane Woodley and Mariah McPhail, with love and thanks for the sex toys and pie recipes; to Valerie King and Andy Maclaurin; to Rosa-Maria DiDonato; to Kim Lane and Austinmama.com. Thanks are due to Katie Allison Granju and the members of her fabulous listserv for "writer mamas" for their advice and camaraderie. Thanks are due to the originators, organizers, and participants of the annual Mama Gathering for all their hard work and ingenuity. I am continually impressed and inspired by the activism of Bee Lavender, Alison Crews, and Julie Cushing to empower and build community among young mothers. Likewise, Andrea Buchanan, Amy Hudock, and the staff of Literarymama.com work tirelessly to give credence to the written lives of mothers. And the Association for Research on Mothering at York University is an invaluable resource for keeping the study of motherhood vital in academia.

Kristin Epley is not a mother, but she is a treasured best friend.

I am indebted to the people who helped connect parts of this book with an audience early in its life. Thanks are due to the staff of *Clamor*, of *Brain, Child*, of *Mamalicious*, of Austinmama.com, of *Crock*, and of *Fertile Ground*. Thanks to the editors I have known—to Maia Rossini, Hilary Flower, Karen Eng, Kate Chynoweth, Catherine Levy, and Candace Walsh. Thanks also to the organizers and participants of Ladyfest Texas 2004. These valuable collaborations reminded me that there is still a need to speak openly about parental depression and the struggles of raising a child; so long as people continue to parent, there always will be.

Thanks are due to my friends at *The Austin Chronicle*, who supported this project and graciously indulged my flakiness during the production process.

Thanks are due to Brooke Warner, my editor, who jumped into this project midstream and acquitted herself with class and verve.

Thanks are due to Briony Scott and Linda Jensen, my sisters in motherhood.

Of special note are the Three Guys Named Jim, indefatigable supporters of my life and work. James Ellis, my webmaster and the only friend I have from high school, is full of brilliant ideas and technical know-how, and he's still into the Next Big Thing before anyone else ever hears of it. James Hornfischer, my tenacious yet personable agent, believed in this book from the beginning and pimped me hardcore. James Ingman, my partner in life and parenting, is simply the Best Guy Ever. He stood by me when the shit rained down, and we came through it together, through long nights of compromised sleep and through long days of anxiety, frustration, and despair. He is a dear and singular person, and I cherish him utterly.

The last word is reserved for Sheila Howard, my mother and friend.

About the Author

MARRIT INGMAN is a regular contributor to *The Austin Chronicle* and *Mamalicious*. Her writing has also been published by *AlterNet; The Anchorage Press; Austinmama. com; Brain, Child; Clamor; The Coast Weekly; Isthmus; Venus;* and other publications. She is a contributor to several Seal Press anthologies, including *The Risks of Sunbathing Topless and Other*

Funny Stories from the Road, Secrets and Confidences: The Complicated Truths about Women's Friendships, and *It's a Boy: Women Writers on Raising Sons.* She has taught at Boston University, Springfield College, and Southwestern University. *Inconsolable* is her first book.

Selected Titles from Seal Press

For more than twenty-five years, Seal Press has published groundbreaking books. By women. For women. Visit our website at www.sealpress.com.

It's a Boy: Women Writers on Raising Sons edited by Andrea J. Buchanan. $14.95, 1-58005-145-6. Seal's edgy take on what it's really like to raise boys, from toddlers to teens and beyond.

I Wanna Be Sedated: 30 Writers on Parenting Teenagers edited by Faith Conlon and Gail Hudson. $15.95, 1-58005-127-8. With hilarious and heartfelt essays from writers such as Dave Barry and Barbara Kingsolver, this anthology will reassure any parent of a teenager that they are not alone.

Reckless: The Outrageous Lives of Nine Kick-Ass Women by Gloria Mattioni. $14.95, 1-58005-148-0. This collection of biographies details the lives of nine women who took unconventional life paths to achieve extraordinary results.

The Unsavvy Traveler: Women's Comic Tales of Catastrophe edited by Rosemary Caperton, Anne Mathews, and Lucie Ocenas. $15.95, 1-58005-142-1. Thirty bitingly funny responses to the question: What happens when trips go wrong?

The Truth behind the Mommy Wars: Who Decides What Makes a Good Mother? by Miriam Peskowitz. $15.95, 1-58005-129-4. This moving and convincing treatise explores the new-century collision between work and mothering.

Toddler: Real-life Stories of Those Fickle, Irrational, Urgent, Tiny People We Love edited by Jennifer Margulis. $14.95, 1-58005-093-X. These clever, succinct, and poignant tales capture all the hilarity, magic, and chaos of raising the complex little people we call toddlers.